radiant visualizations

bear

Marilyne Verschueren

ming

CHRONICLE BOOKS
SAN FRANCISCO

to expand your mind and open your heart

Dedication

This book is dedicated to you. If you are reading this,
thank you, truly, from the bottom of my heart. I'm so
grateful that my art somehow made its way to you,
wherever you are in the world. My biggest hope is that
you find comfort and peace within these pages.
That the colors and shapes bring you inspiration
and that the text reminds you of things we all forget
along the way. I hope these pages offer you moments
of awe and light, reminding you of all the beautiful
possibilities that await you.

xx Marilyne

Library of Congress Cataloging-in-Publication Data available.

ISBN 978-1-7972-2816-7

Manufactured in China.

10 9 8 7 6 5 4 3 2 1

Chronicle books and gifts are available at special quantity discounts
to corporations, professional associations, literacy programs, and other
organizations. For details and discount information, please contact our
premiums department at corporatesales@chroniclebooks.com or
at 1-800-759-0190.

Chronicle Books LLC
680 Second Street
San Francisco, California 94107
www.chroniclebooks.com

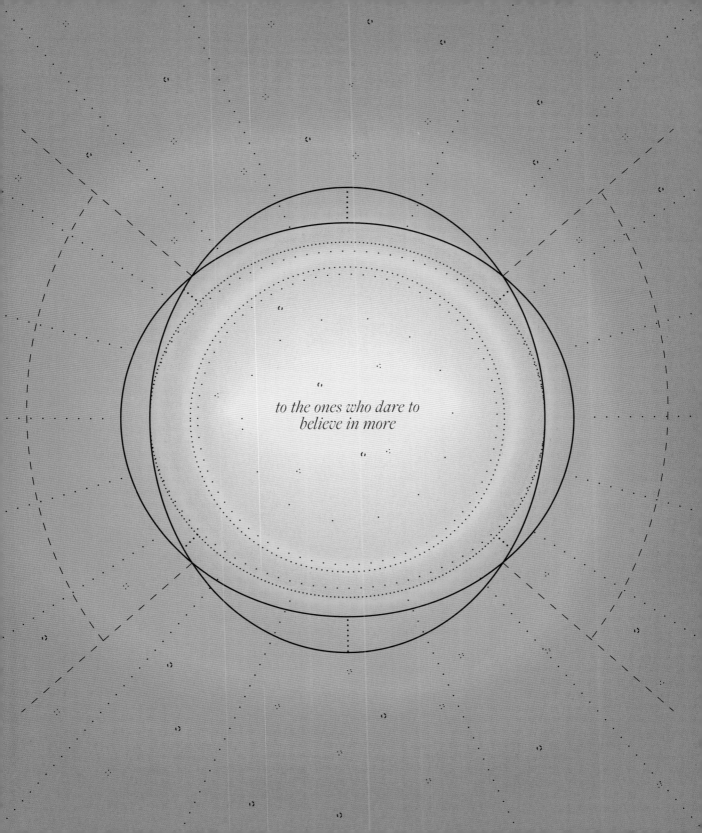

*to the ones who dare to
believe in more*

Contents

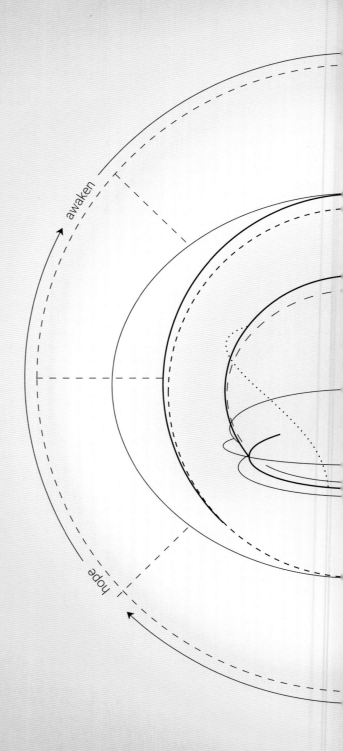

awaken

hope

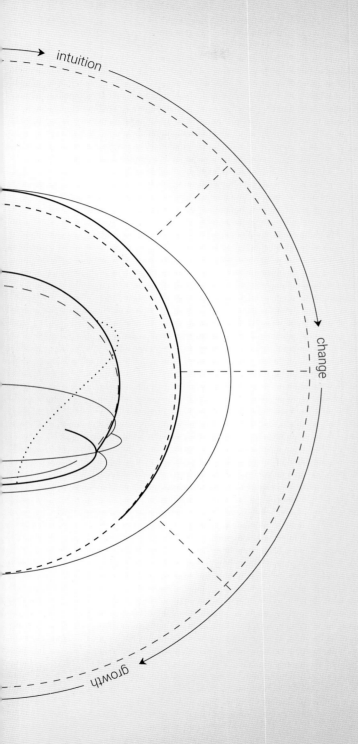

intuition

change

growth

Introduction

I believe we are all here for a reason. That we each have an individual purpose and a collective purpose in this thing called life. This collective experience unites us. Our individual paths may look different—we're born in separate bodies, in different families, and in different parts of the world, but still, we are all on a journey to uncover the same universal truths. And to really learn these truths, we have to experience the journey firsthand.

As we explore what it means to be a human being in this world, we discover that we are all connected to something deeper and greater than ourselves. If we take a moment to observe our surroundings, we witness the presence of miracles all around us—in nature, in humanity, or in the great unknown. When we pay attention, we see that life is not as ordinary as we think it is. This sense of wonder is something we are connected to in childhood— the excitement that comes with each day, the sense of playfulness and possibility in each experience. When we were children, everything looked brighter. Everything was alive. Everything was magical. We were absolutely and unconditionally in love with life.

For most of us, this sense of love and wonder has faded away over time. But losing that perspective makes it all the more amazing to rediscover. We have to experience the dark to appreciate the light. We have to go through hard times to grow as people. We have to weather these storms to discover our true selves and our purposes.

As you move through life, you will face choices, and every decision you make will steer you in a certain way. These decisions are the wind in your sail. And as you navigate life's rough waters and calm seas, a voice will follow you wherever you go. This is your inner compass guiding you to your true north. It will nudge you toward what feels right and warn you when something feels off. It is there, with you, to guide you and help you fulfill your calling here on Earth.

Art can support us in this lifelong journey, offering us opportunities for deep contemplation and awareness that help us connect with our intuition. I believe that I am here to uplift people on their life paths through my art, and I started Beamingdesign to share visual reminders of hope, love, and empathy. Through that experience, I've connected with thousands of people around the world who are eager for positive messages that offer them moments of beauty and connection.

This book is a collection of my work, including pieces I've shared online and never-before-seen artwork. The content is organized into five sections designed to take you on a spiritual journey of self-discovery, from awakening to hope. You'll also find short practices for meditation, breath work, journaling, and more woven in to these pages to offer you simple ways to deepen your experience.

There is no right or wrong way to approach this book. Open it to a random page, or read it from front to back, chapter by chapter. You can turn to it when you need a moment of joy, or make a practice out of looking at the start of each day to begin it with hope and light. The content is designed to be flexible and adaptable, allowing you to navigate it in a way that feels most meaningful.

Art is a deeply personal experience, and I encourage you to experience this book in your own unique way. You may be drawn to certain colors, or you may connect with a particular message. This is the true beauty of art: It speaks to each heart differently, and it has the power to evoke a wide range of emotions within us.

This book is ultimately meant to serve as a beacon of hope and positivity, offering you a source of inspiration and motivation whenever you may need it. My hope is to uplift you and make you feel less alone. I hope my art reminds you that you are here for a reason and that life is an extraordinary journey worth living. I hope it inspires you to see the world in a new light and embrace new experiences as they arise, knowing they will help you grow and expand your horizons.

Above all, my hope is that *Beaming* rekindles your sense of wonder and love for life and that it supports you on your journey to greater happiness and joy.

Marilyne

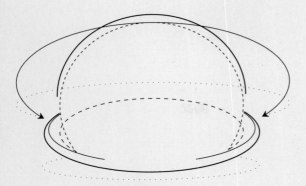

if you are seeking a sign,
you can open this book to any page

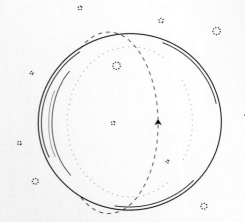

the colors and diagrams provide
space for your mind to wander

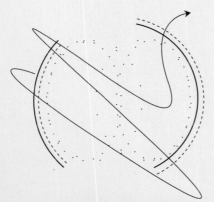

keep your favorite page open
on your coffee table

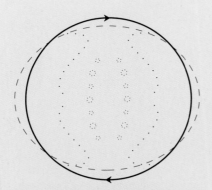

take a pencil, add additional thoughts
or ideas you don't want to forget

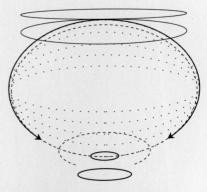

find a quiet space in nature
to read this book

Chapter 1

Awaken

Have you ever had a transformative moment, when you suddenly realize that there must be more to life? Maybe you went through a life event that sparked a new way of thinking or a change in direction. Perhaps you witnessed an act of kindness that had a deep impact on you. For some people, this moment happens in an instant, and for others, it's a slower journey to awakening. These awakenings can lead you to question everything around you or wonder if life will ever be the same.

An awakening can prompt you to question your values, beliefs, or outlook. It may lead you to wonder who you really are, why you're here, and how you can lead a meaningful and fulfilling life. These moments can be incredible opportunities to consider what brings you true joy and fulfillment and what legacy you want to leave behind.

Pay attention to the moments that light you up: They are gifts that move you toward awareness and allow you to act with intention. When you are truly awake, you can appreciate the beauty and complexity of life and better understand your role and purpose in this universe.

the universe *talks* to you

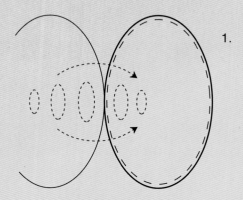

1.

it sends you subtle messages

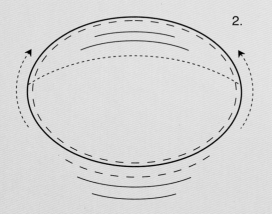

2.

it gives you gut feelings

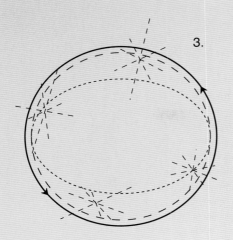

3.

it shows you signs

4.

it responds to your frequency

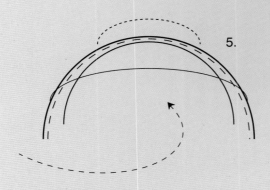

5.

it leads you onto new paths

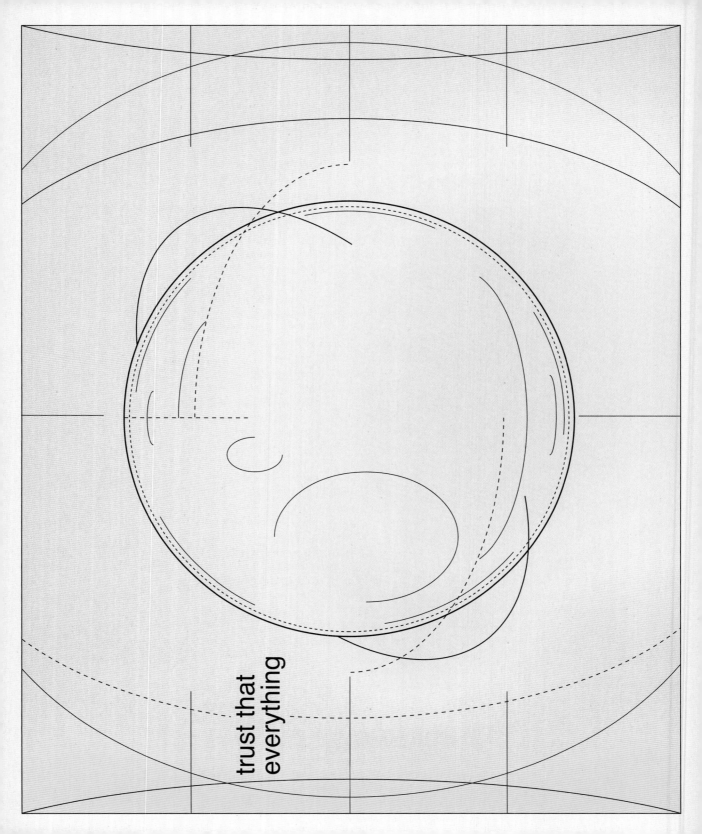

trust that
everything

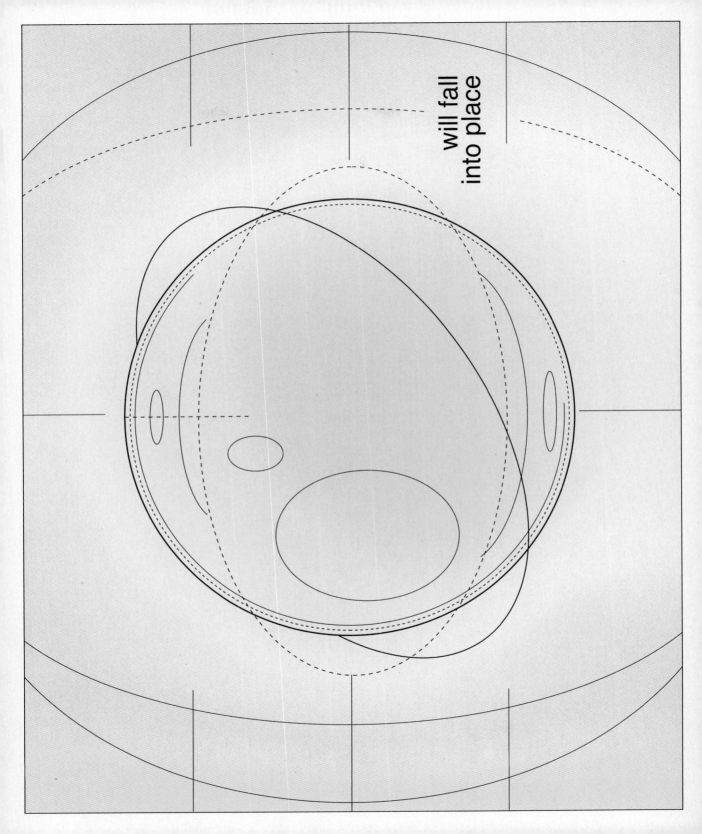

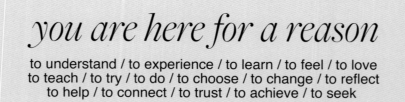

you are here for a reason

to understand / to experience / to learn / to feel / to love
to teach / to try / to do / to choose / to change / to reflect
to help / to connect / to trust / to achieve / to seek

everything is going to be *okay*

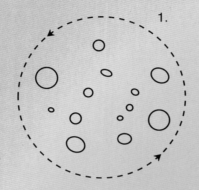

1.

there is still so much future

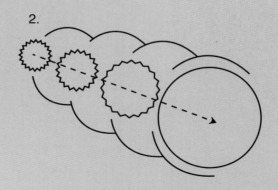

2.

good things are coming

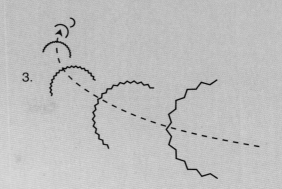

feelings are temporary

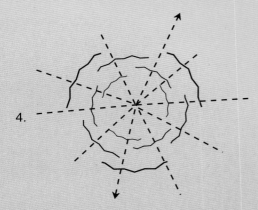

after the rain there is sunshine

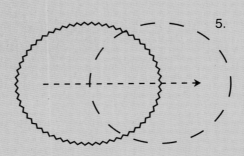

endings are often beautiful beginnings in disguise

I am one with the universe. nature teaches me, the sun energizes me, the moon protects me, and the stars guide me.

see the beauty

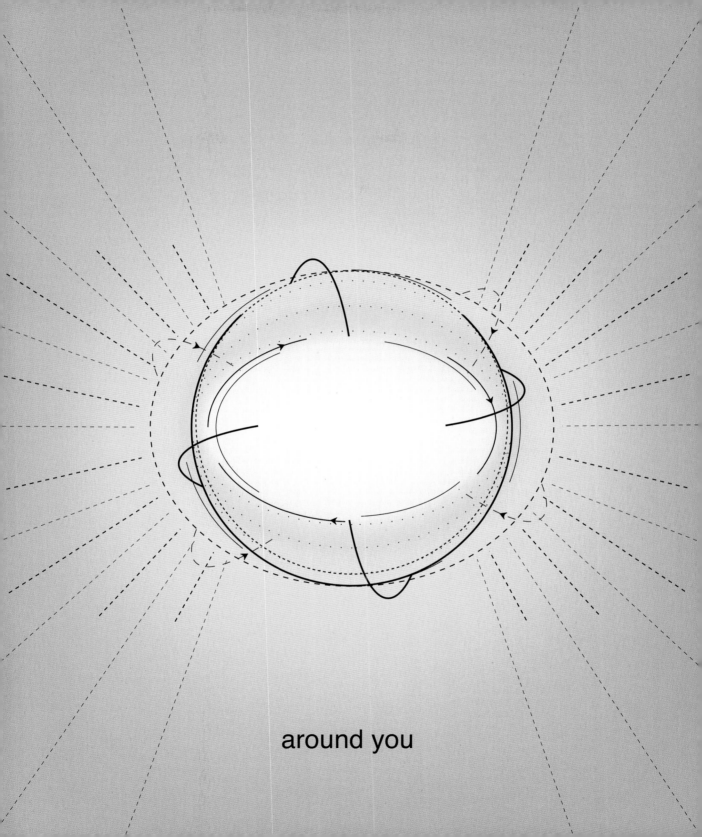

around you

signs from
the universe

Signs can offer comfort and guidance to many individuals,
providing a sense of reassurance and direction in life.
For those who believe in them, signs can hold significant
meaning and value. Look around and within you. Do you
see them? Do you recognize your signs?

1. dreams

4. unexpected opportunities

5. sense of clarity and peace

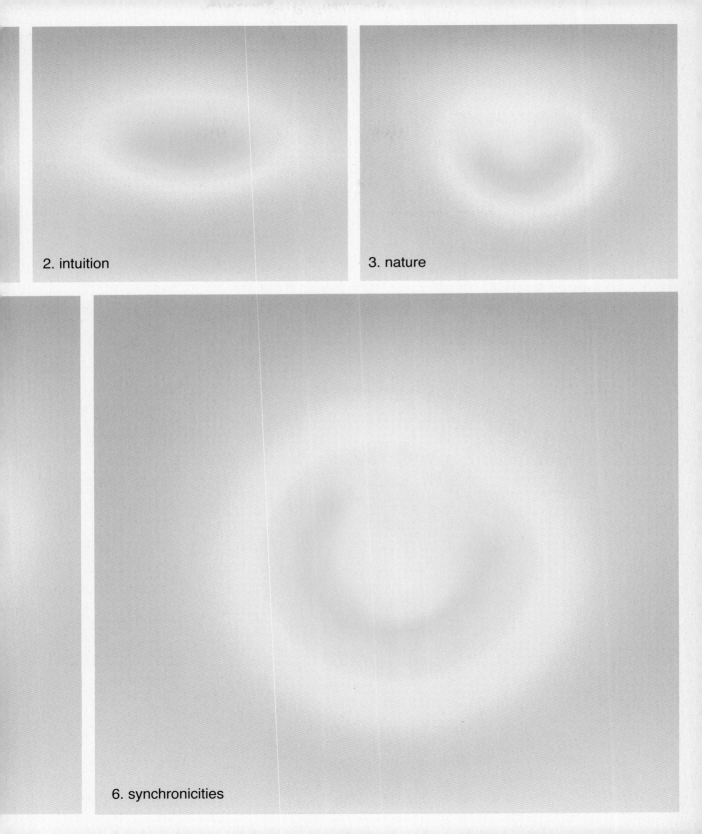

2. intuition

3. nature

6. synchronicities

in the

be

1. Begin your day with gratitude by focusing on the things you're thankful for.
2. Savor your favorite beverage and enjoy the moment.
3. Step outside and take a moment to soak up the warmth of the sun on your skin.

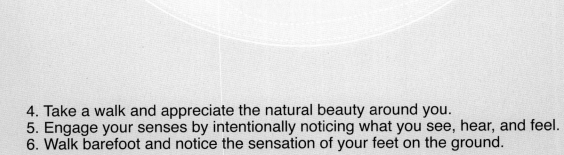

now

4. Take a walk and appreciate the natural beauty around you.
5. Engage your senses by intentionally noticing what you see, hear, and feel.
6. Walk barefoot and notice the sensation of your feet on the ground.

Daily reminders for a great day
(to read every morning)

1. The real joys in life are simple things.

2. Find sweetness in the bitter; find happiness in challenging moments.

3. Be grateful for what you already have.

4. Life isn't long; make those memories.

5. Be a warm person; radiate hope and light.

6. Life is not a race; do things at your own pace.

7. Forgive yourself for the burden of not knowing what you haven't yet learned.

8. Seek reasons to smile and find moments of joy today.

every day has the
potential to become
the best of your life

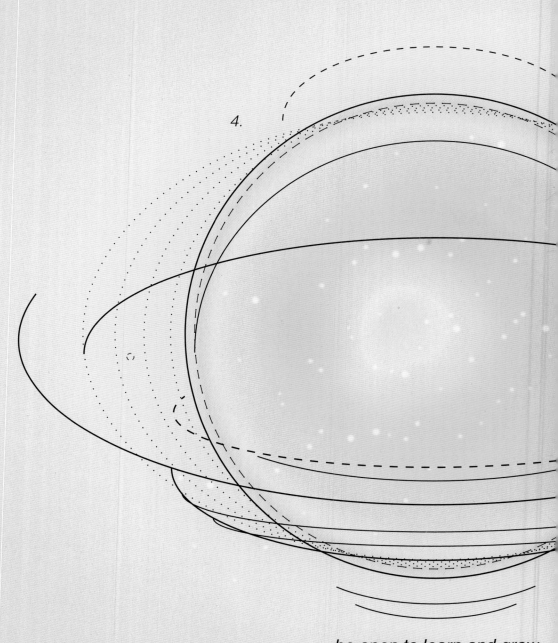

4.

be open to learn and grow

the journey of *self-discovery*

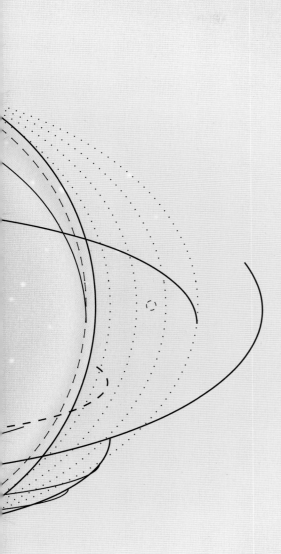

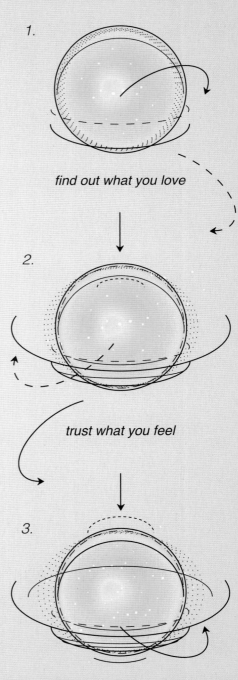

1.

find out what you love

2.

trust what you feel

3.

know what you need

love is

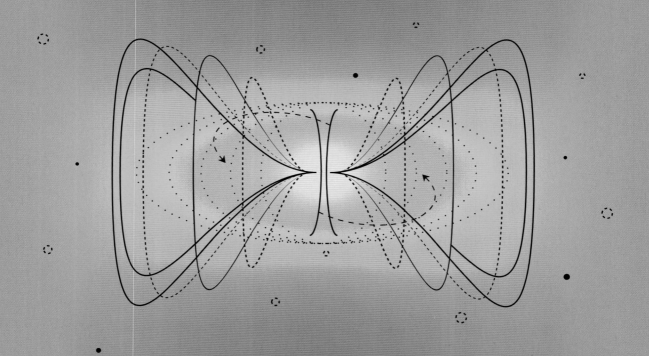

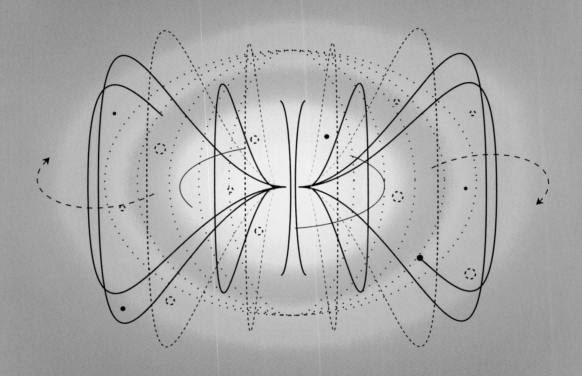

the highest vibration in the universe

the world is grateful to have you

life is not always easy, but don't give up

you are
unique

everyone has a reason for being here

your journey is special; you are one of billions

heart and mind
conversations

heart and mind

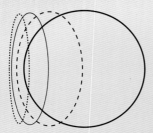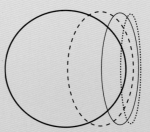

making contact

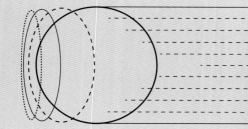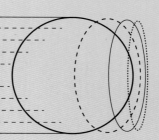

a conversation

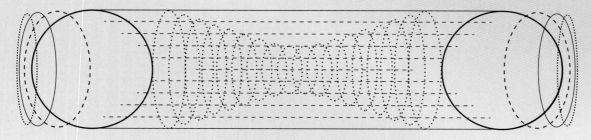

Is this what I want?	*Is this what I stand for?*
What do I want in life?	*How does this feel to me?*
Is this something for me?	*Why am I feeling this way?*

An inner conversation
for clarity and balance

1. Imagine your heart as a beautiful, glowing light.

2. Bring your attention to the forefront of your mind.

3. Begin the conversation by asking your heart what it feels about a particular situation or decision.

4. Allow yourself to feel the emotions that arise.

5. Then, ask your mind for its perspective. Allow yourself to think logically and objectively about the situation.

6. Allow the conversation to flow naturally, moving back and forth between your heart and your mind. You may notice that your heart and mind have different viewpoints, and that's OK.

7. Listen carefully to your heart and your mind, and try to find a middle ground where both can be satisfied.

8. When you feel ready, take a few deep breaths. Consider what action you can take based on the conversation. Trust your decision.

a life full
of *meaning*

experiencing
new things

loving
others

living in
the moment

finding a
passion

giving
back

taking it all in

making a
difference

wanting to
evolve

enjoy the present

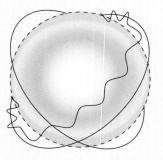

pause for a moment

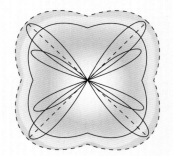

connect on a deeper level

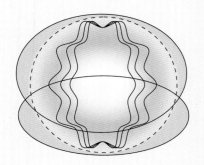

take a
moment to

appreciate where you are

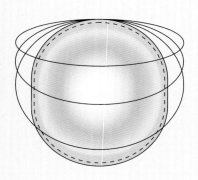

send positive energy

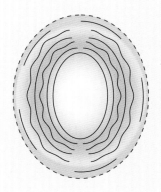

carry out an act of kindness

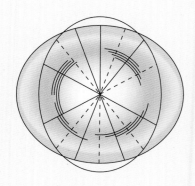

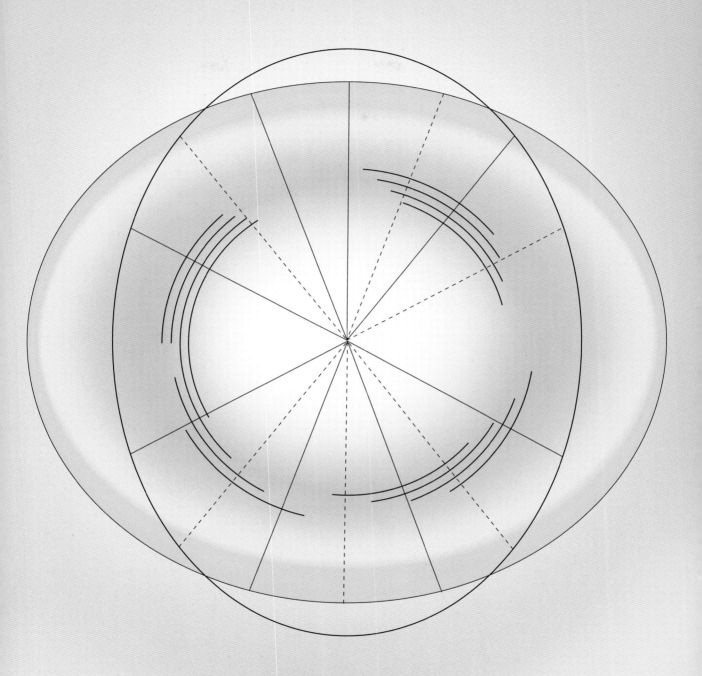

Chapter 2

Intuition

Your intuition is the compass that guides you to your true north, toward your passion and purpose. It's the voice that speaks to you through the noise of the world, nudging you toward what feels right and warning you against what feels wrong. When you follow your intuition, you feel a sense of exhilaration and freedom; when you ignore it, you feel a weight in your stomach.

It takes practice to tune in to this inner voice. By paying attention to the things that bring you joy and fulfillment, you can learn to make decisions in alignment with your truth and recognize the signs that you're on the right path.

In a world that's often loud and chaotic, it's easy to get swept up in other people's opinions and lose sight of your own inner voice. Taking time to be alone, to breathe, and to listen to your intuition is essential for finding your way. Trusting yourself is a process, but by building self-awareness and cultivating a deep connection to your intuition, you'll find the clarity and direction you need to live a fulfilling and authentic life.

trust

your

magic

gut feelings

1. deep knowing of what to do

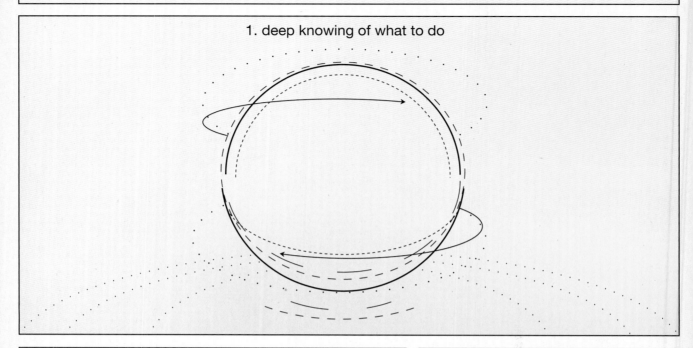

2. vivid dreams

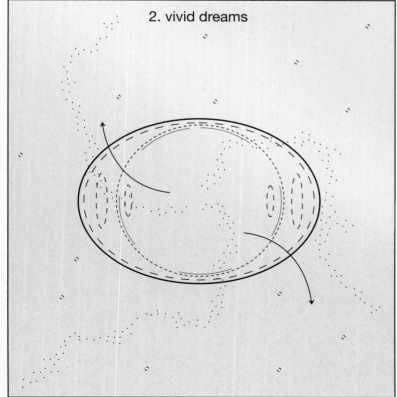

3. stomach feelings (good and bad)

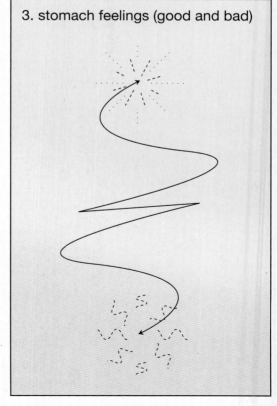

4. noticing patterns

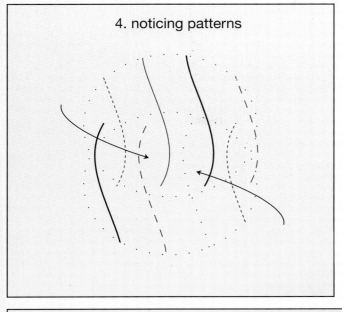

5. sense of clarity

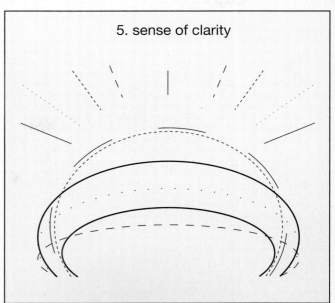

6. synchronicities

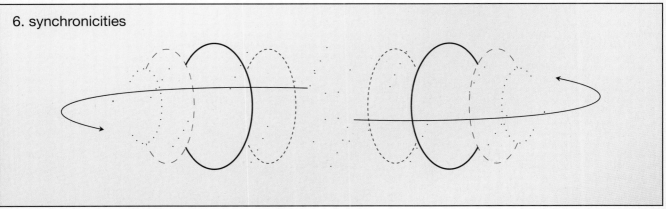

7. feeling of being guided in a direction

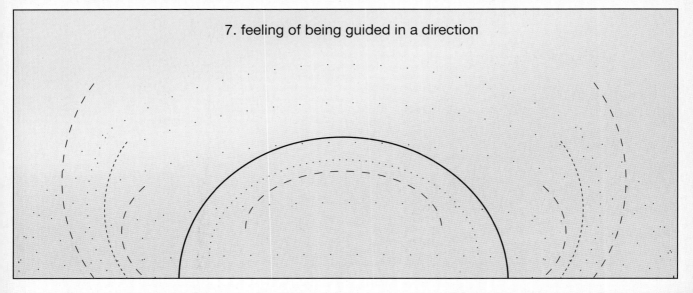

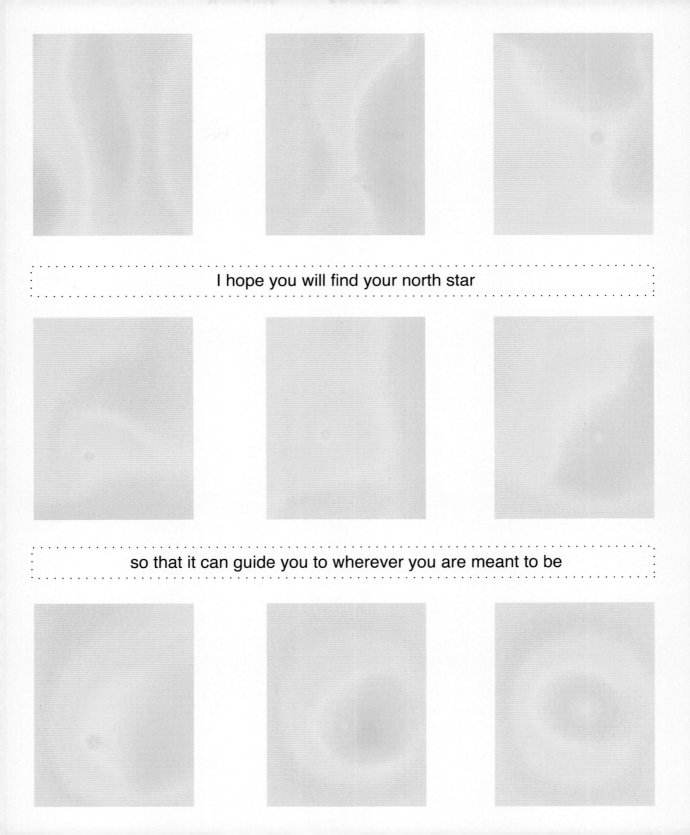

I hope you will find your north star

so that it can guide you to wherever you are meant to be

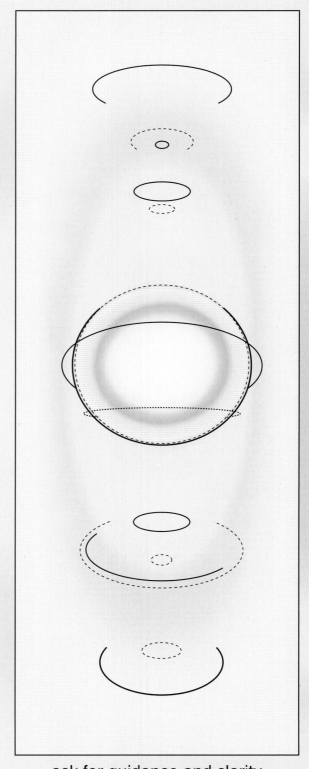

ask for guidance and clarity

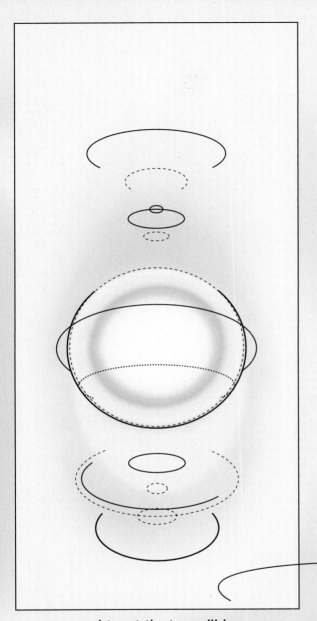

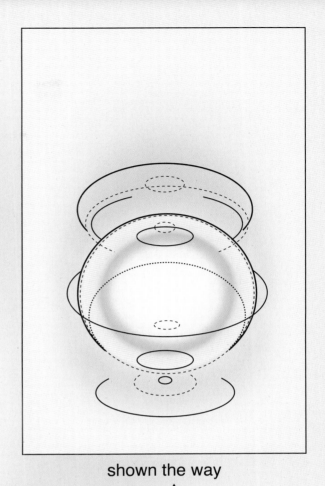

shown the way

and trust that you'll be

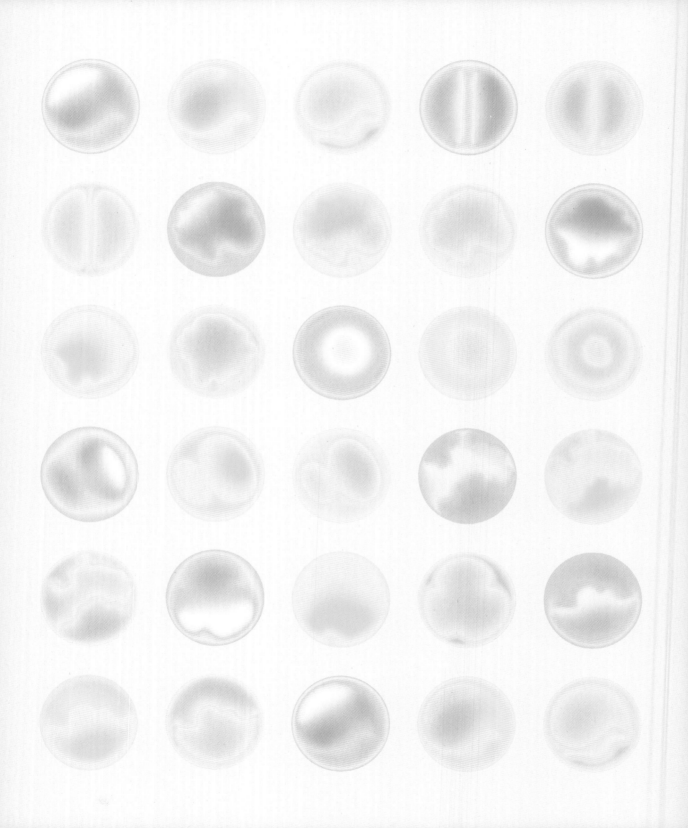

meaningful things

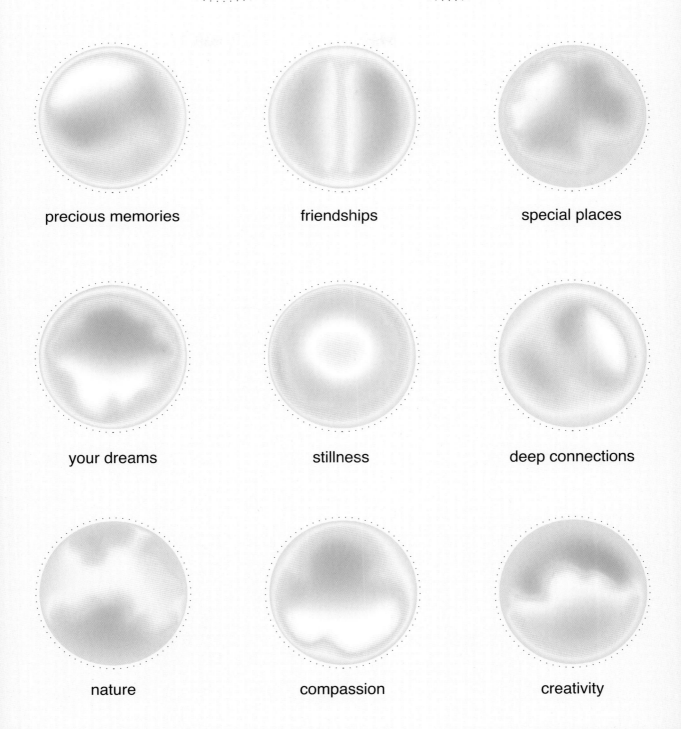

precious memories

friendships

special places

your dreams

stillness

deep connections

nature

compassion

creativity

take time for yourself

Believe and receive

1. Believe in yourself and your abilities.

2. Listen to your heart and intuition. Your inner voice can guide you toward what you truly want in life.

3. Ask for guidance and support from your higher power to help you achieve your goals.

4. Cultivate positive thoughts and optimism by focusing on the good things and people in your life.

5. Trust that the universe is helping you in ways you may not be aware of.

6. Finally, express gratitude and maintain a positive outlook. Gratitude attracts more positivity and abundance into your life.

you are on your way

look how far you've come

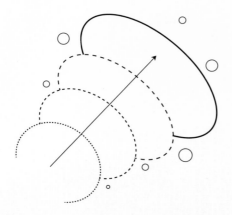

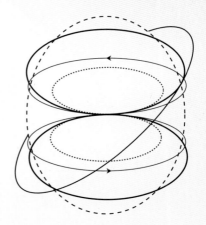

believe to
receive

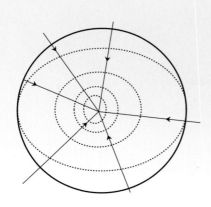

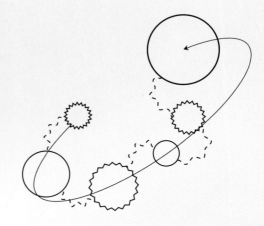

trust your inner voice

rewire your thoughts daily

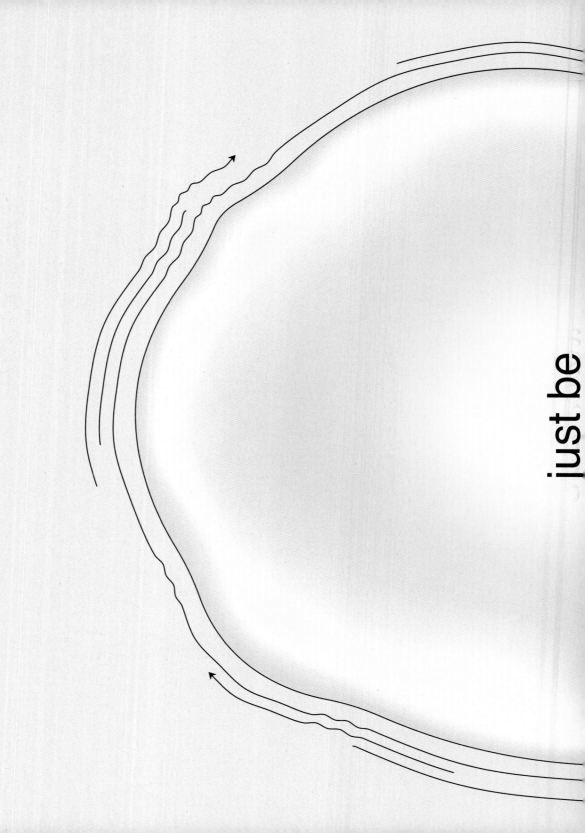

just be

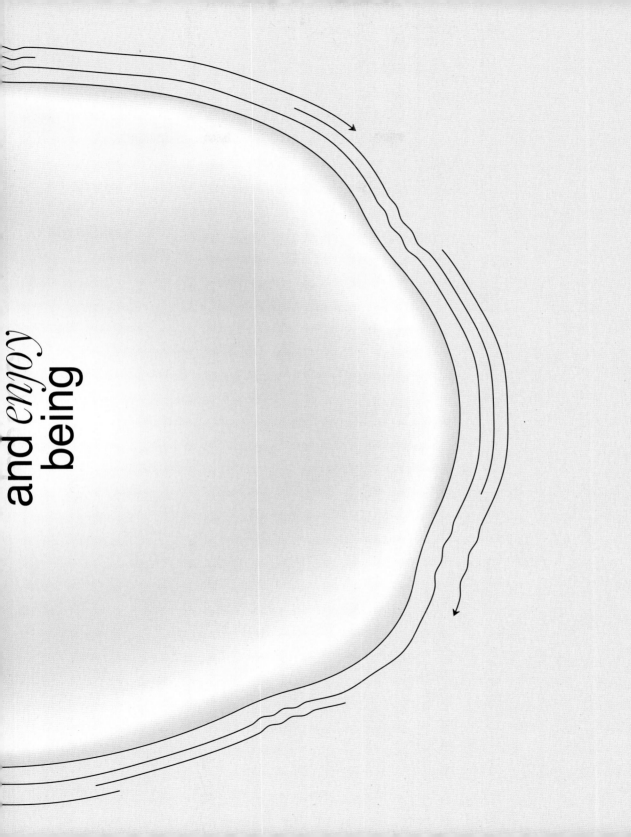

and *enjoy* being

1.

2.

3.

4.

5.

what's meant
for you
will *always*
find you

6.

7.

8.

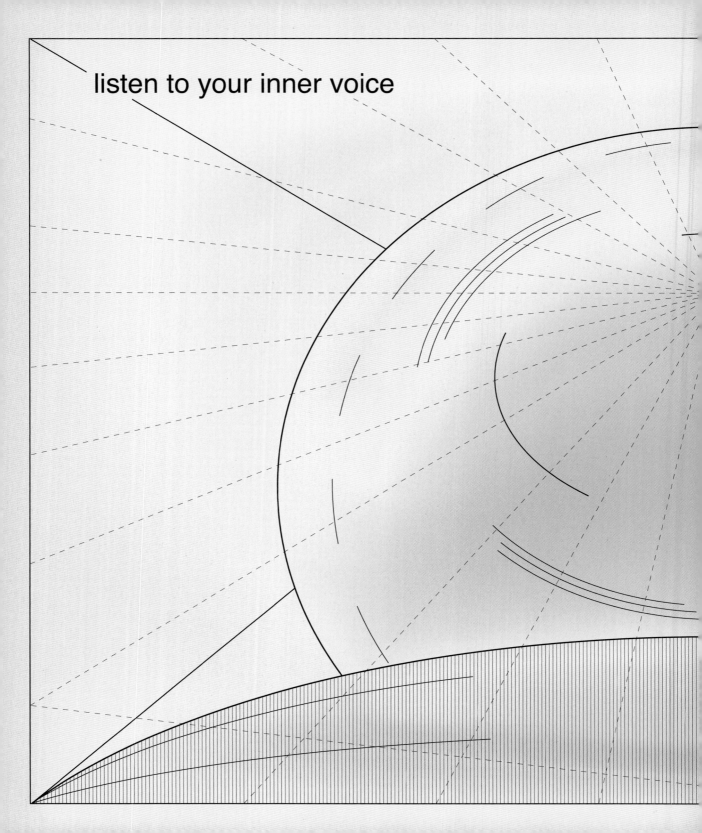

listen to your inner voice

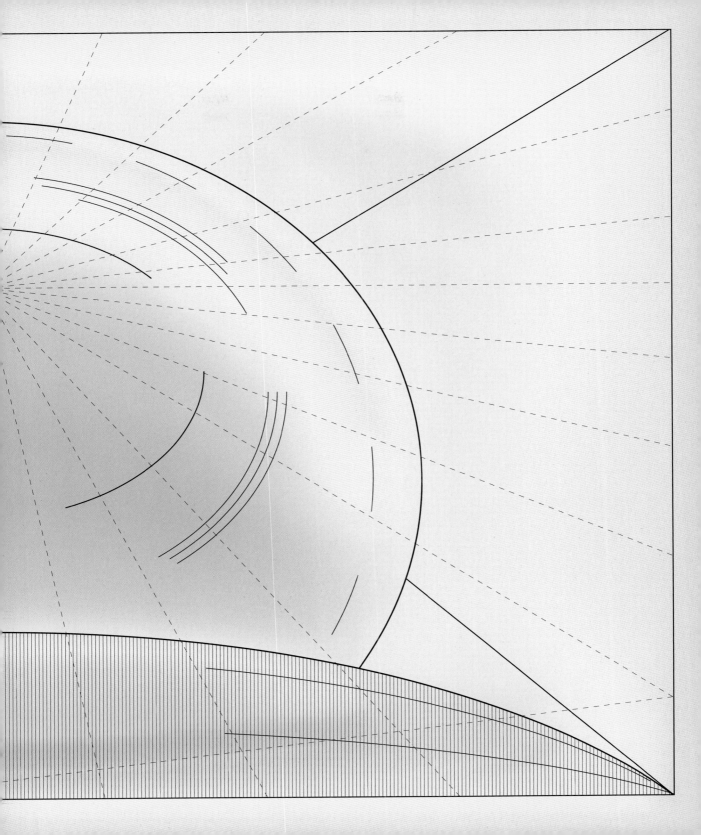

inhale all the good

kindness - compassion - generosity - gratitude - honesty - respect - empathy - joy

exhale all the bad

distrust - indifference - stinginess - ingratitude - dishonesty - impatience - disrespect - sadness

do what

Makes your
heart smile

Discover what brings joy to your heart:

Take a piece of paper and draw three overlapping circles.

In the first circle, jot down the things that you are naturally drawn to.
In the second circle, write down the things that you love to do.
In the third circle, list the things that you are deeply passionate about.

The first circle is connected to your life purpose, the second circle to your life path, and the third circle to your life passion.

All three circles are connected to your overall happiness. Ask yourself, *What would be possible if I blended these three things together?*

how to practice stillness

Go outside,
find a spot to sit down,
or go for a walk.

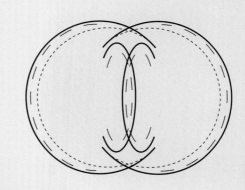

When you feel relaxed,
you can enjoy the space you are in.

Enjoy the quietness.
Enjoy the sun on your face
and the wind in your hair.

Enjoy being.

Stillness is a state of calmness, in which you feel relaxed and peaceful. Creating moments of stillness allows you to reconnect with yourself.

Relax your body and quiet your mind by repeating calming phrases.

Everything is OK.
I am doing great.
My heart feels light.
I feel peaceful.
I am calm.

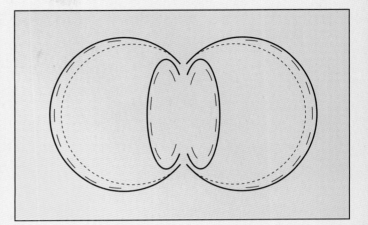

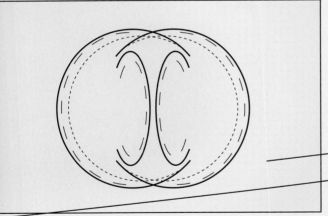

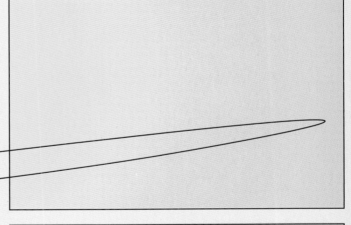

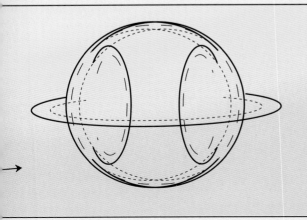

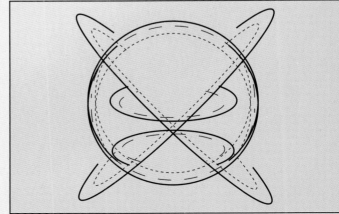

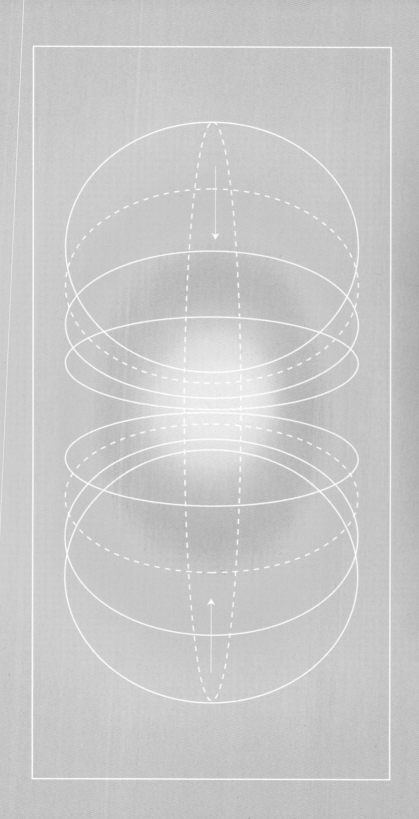

tap into the *voice* of your intuition

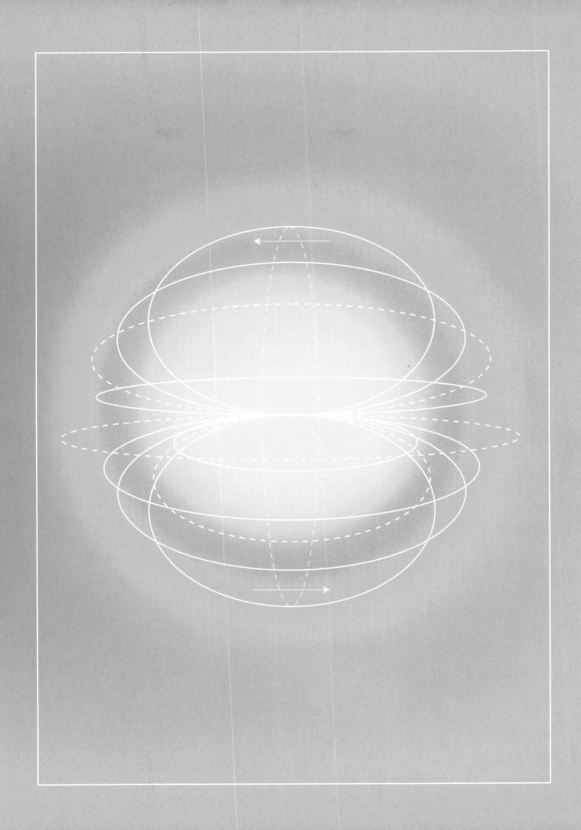

create

visualize

attract

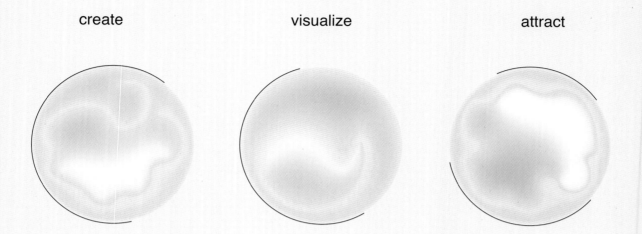

use your
thoughts to

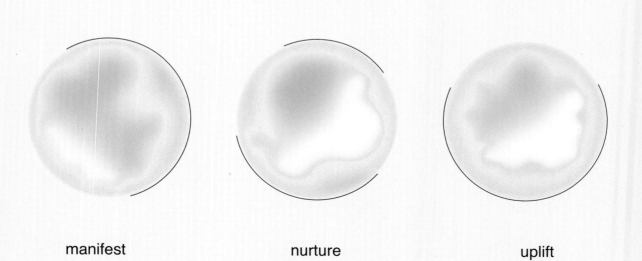

manifest

nurture

uplift

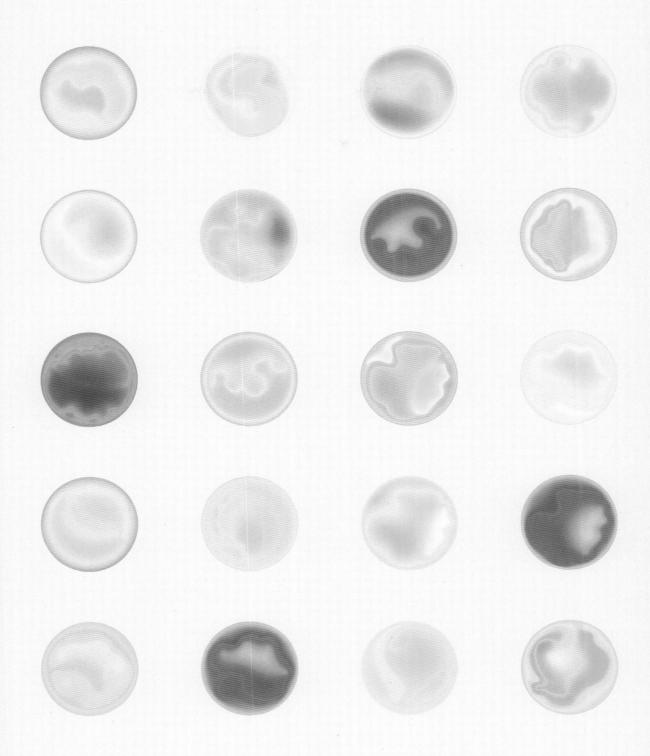

take care of your energy

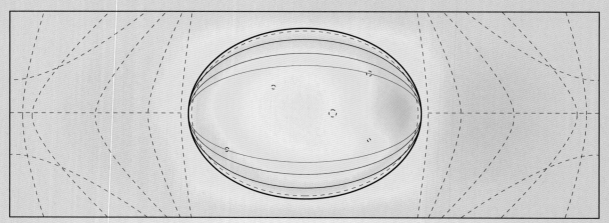

if it feels authentic and true to you,

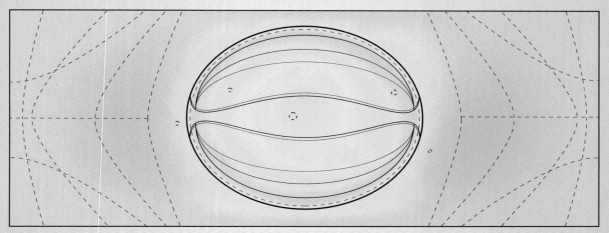

you're on the right path

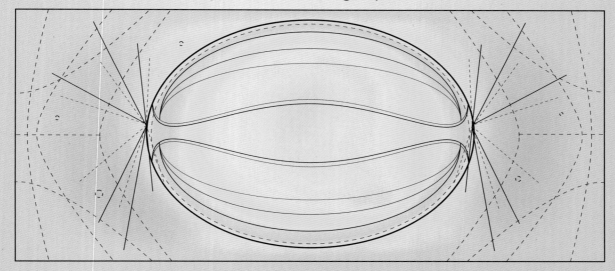

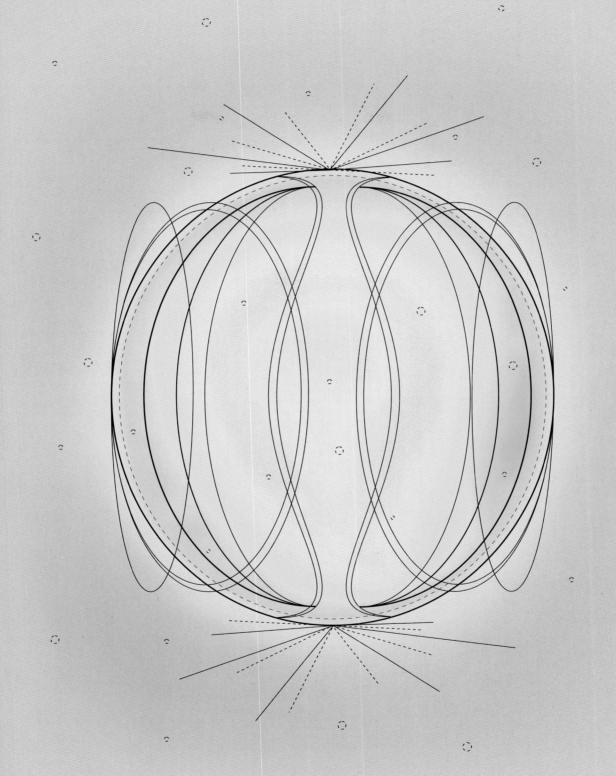

79

I am protected
I choose prosperity
I love and accept myself
I am allowed to take time
I am blessed

affirm

Recharge your soul

1. Take a warm and soothing shower, allowing the water to wash away any tension or negative energy.

2. As you stand under the water, imagine it cleansing your body and revitalizing your spirit.

3. Take deep breaths and visualize any stress or worries being washed away, replaced by a sense of calm.

4. Embrace the peacefulness of the moment, letting go of any external distractions.

5. After the shower, wrap yourself in a cozy blanket and find a comfortable place to sit or lie down.

6. Allow yourself to relax completely, surrendering to the safety and warmth of your surroundings.

7. Take deep, slow breaths, focusing on each inhale and exhale, allowing yourself to unwind and recharge.

8. Stay in this tranquil state for as long as needed, letting your body and mind replenish their energy.

loves
nature

is
deeply
intuitive

needs
alone time

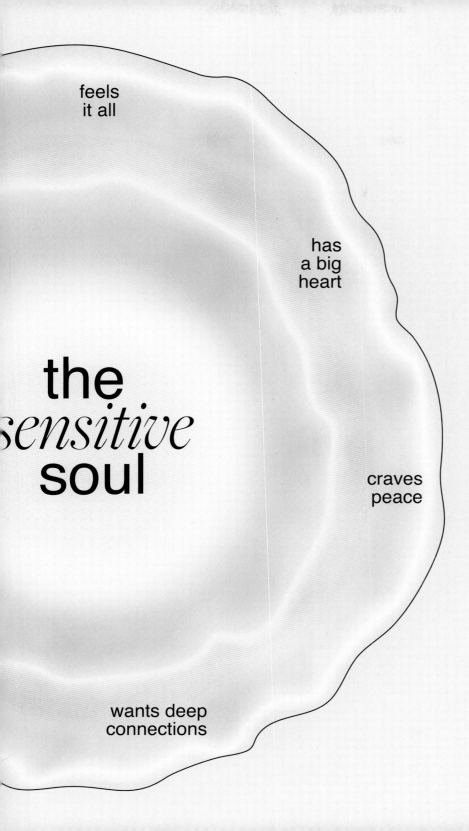

feels
it all

has
a big
heart

the
sensitive
soul

craves
peace

wants deep
connections

Chapter 3

Change

Change is an inevitable part of life. Like the cycles of nature, we too go through seasons—nothing in life is stagnant. It can be scary or overwhelming to have to start over or leave behind what we know, but change is an opportunity for growth and renewal. When we embrace it with an open mind and heart, it can lead us to beautiful new possibilities and eye-opening experiences.

Change also offers us a chance to approach things in a fresh way, applying the new perspectives and insights we have gained on our journey. We may discover strengths and abilities we never knew we had. When we begin to view change as an opportunity, we give ourselves the chance to grow and flourish. Embrace change and all it brings. Trust that it will lead you to where you need to be.

just like the

sun,

we have light within us

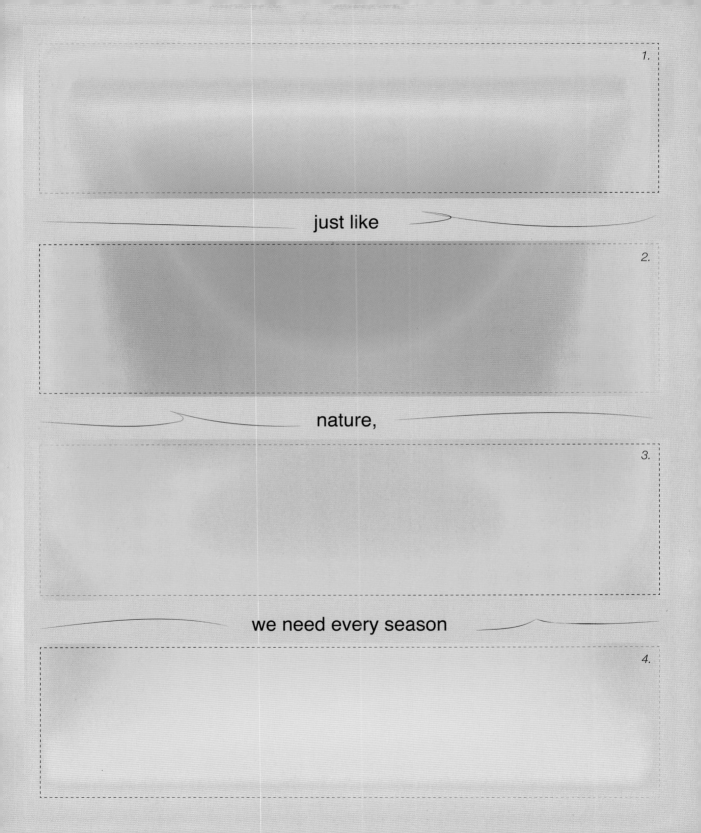

1.

just like

2.

nature,

3.

we need every season

4.

life unfolds organically and naturally . . .

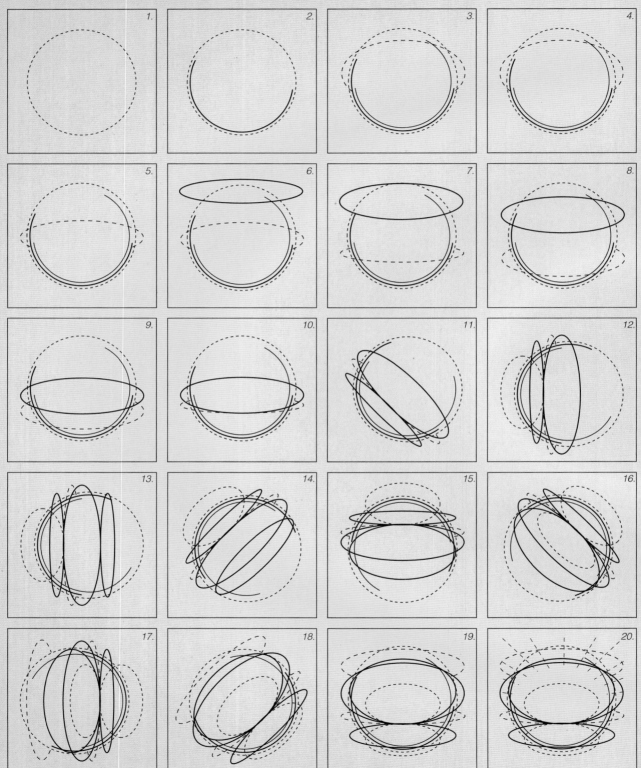

always and forever changing

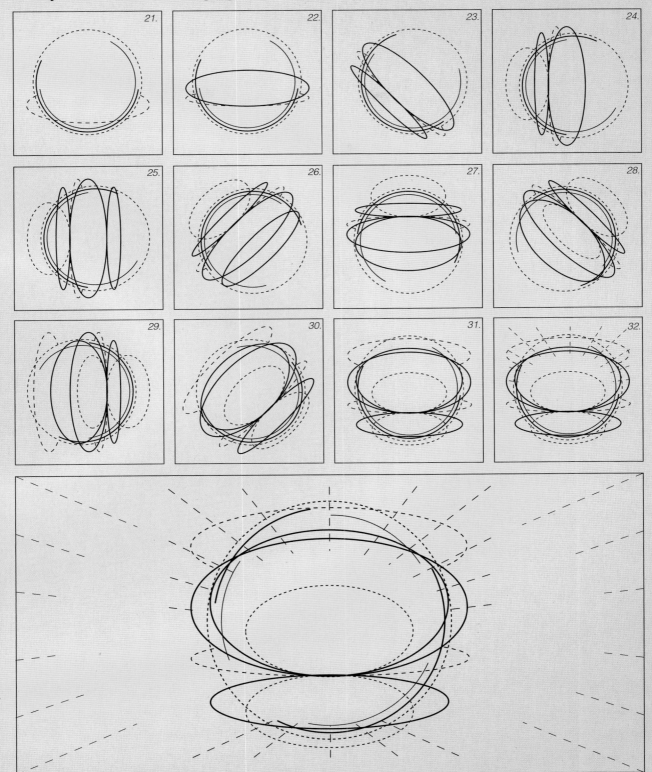

chapters of life

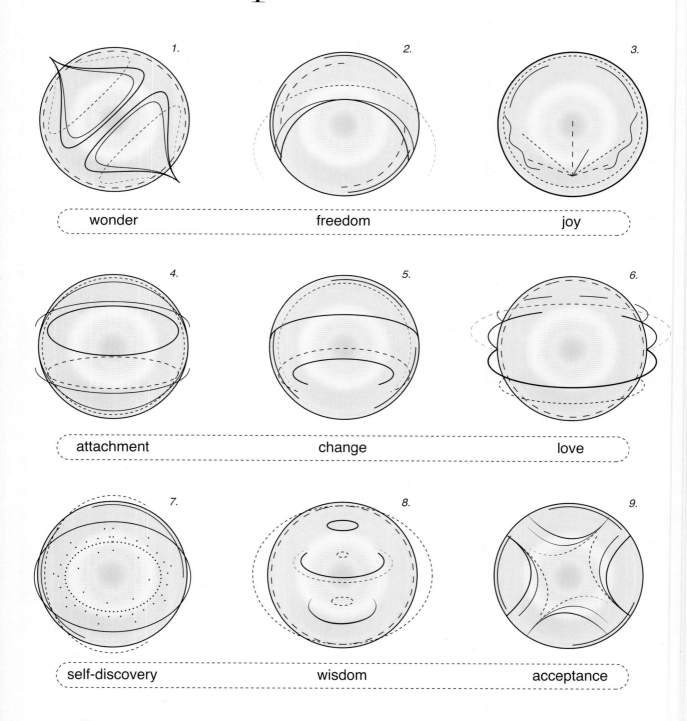

1. wonder
2. freedom
3. joy
4. attachment
5. change
6. love
7. self-discovery
8. wisdom
9. acceptance

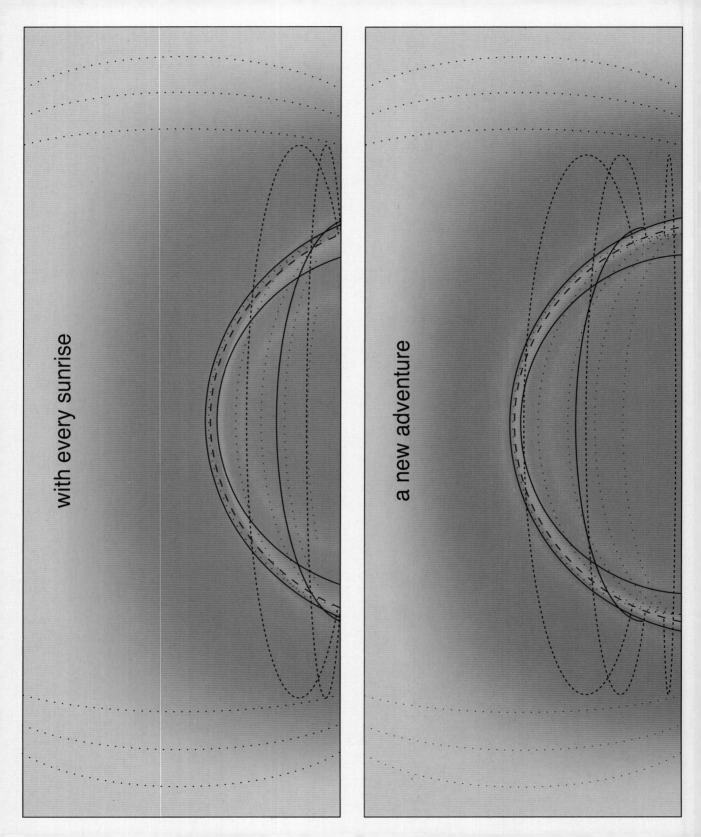

awaits you

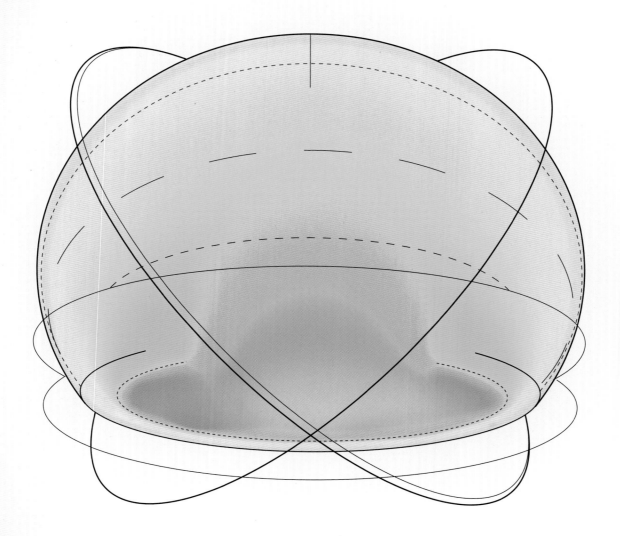

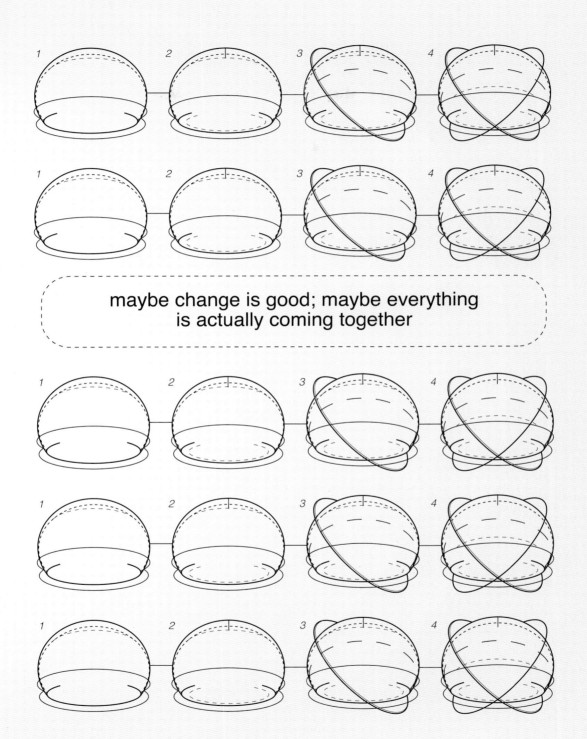

maybe change is good; maybe everything
is actually coming together

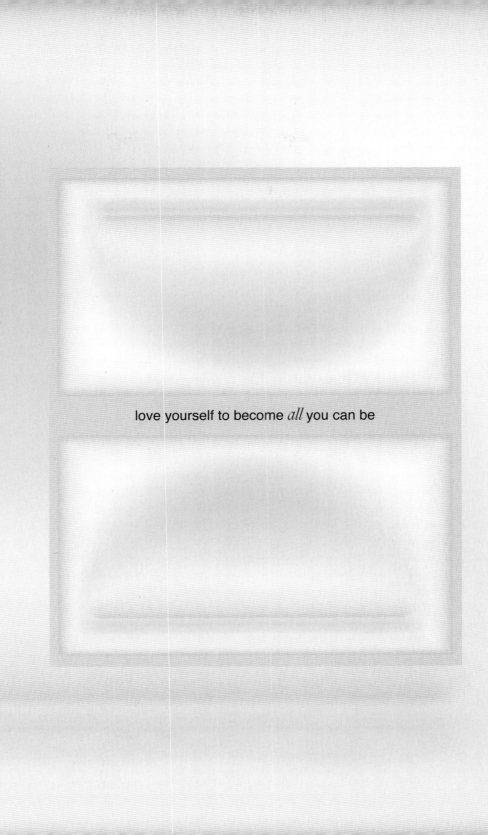

love yourself to become *all* you can be

a mantra

I accept myself as I am,

with all my strengths

and weaknesses.

I know I'm not perfect,

but that's OK

because

it gives me room

to grow and

to improve.

My flaws don't make me

who I am, but they do

help me become

a better version of myself.

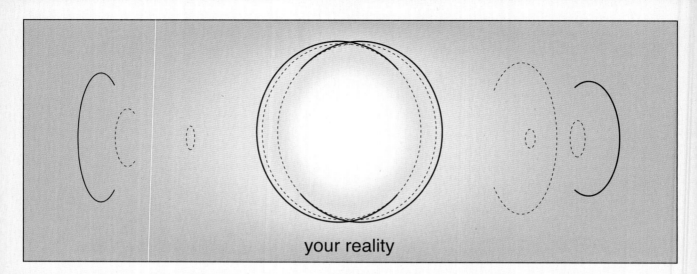
your reality

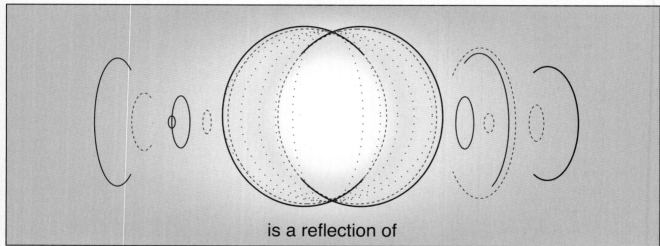
is a reflection of

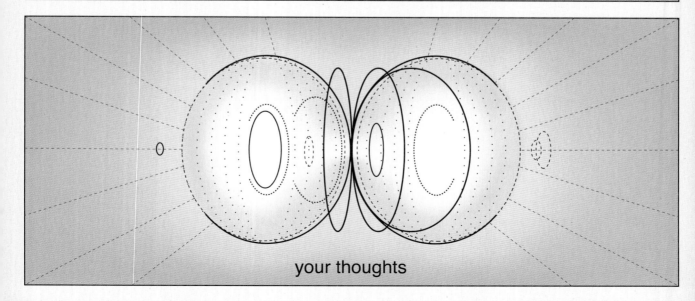
your thoughts

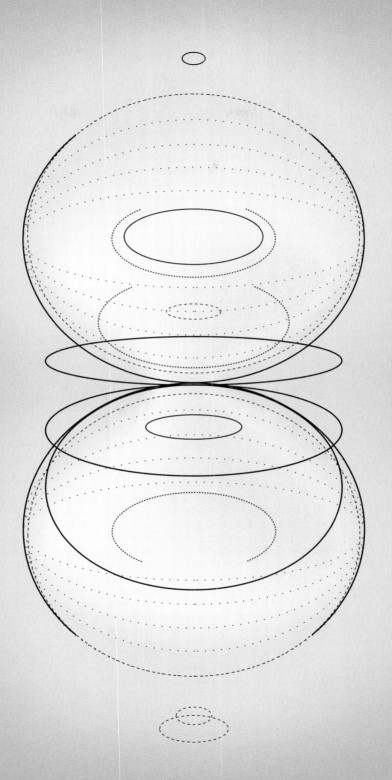

a *grateful* heart

trusts the universe

believes in goodness

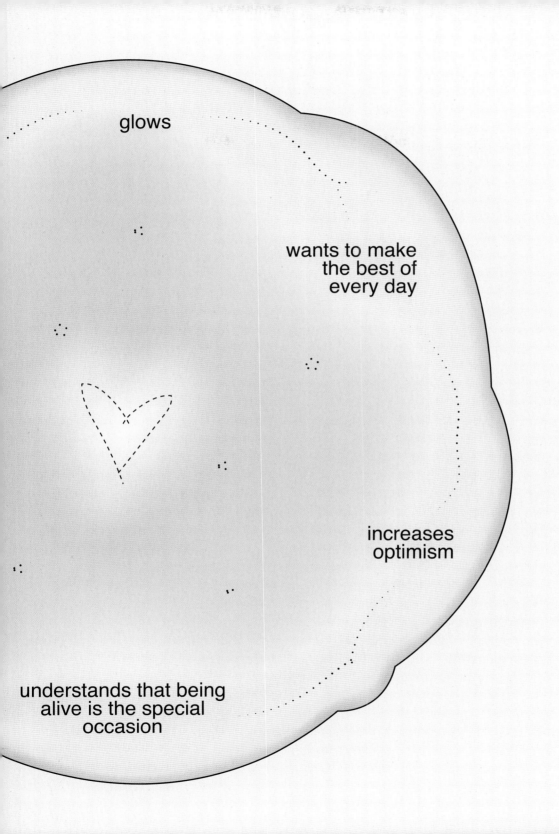

glows

wants to make
the best of
every day

increases
optimism

understands that being
alive is the special
occasion

uplift your energy

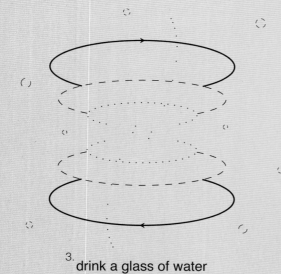

1. put on your favorite
   upbeat song

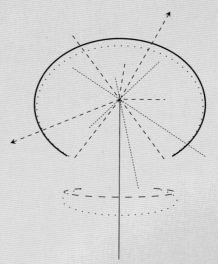

2. dance and move
   your body

3. drink a glass of water

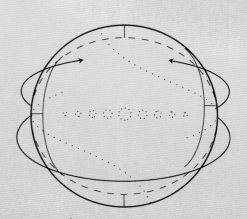

4. step outside and
   inhale fresh air

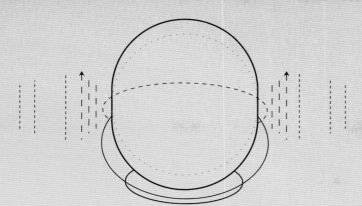

5.
find a place to sit and
soak up rays of sunshine

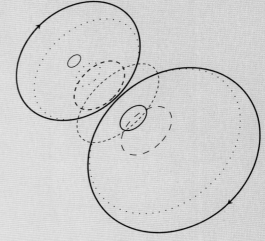

6.
lie down on the grass and feel
a connection to the earth

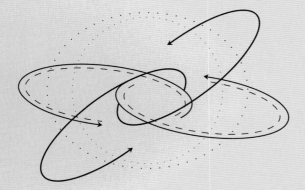

7.
look up at the sky and
let go of all your worries

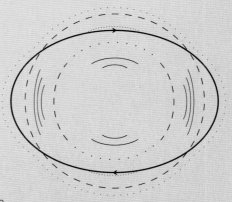

8.
allow yourself to feel a connection
to something greater than yourself

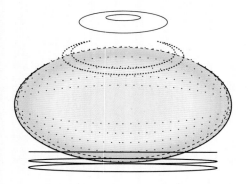

1. the start of a new chapter

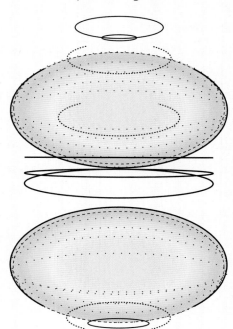

2. personal growth

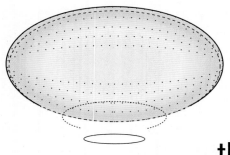

the *benefits* of change

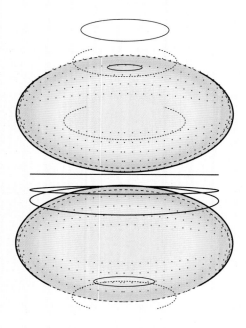

3. new opportunities

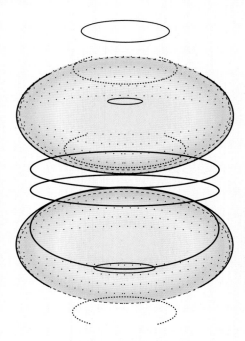

4. resilience

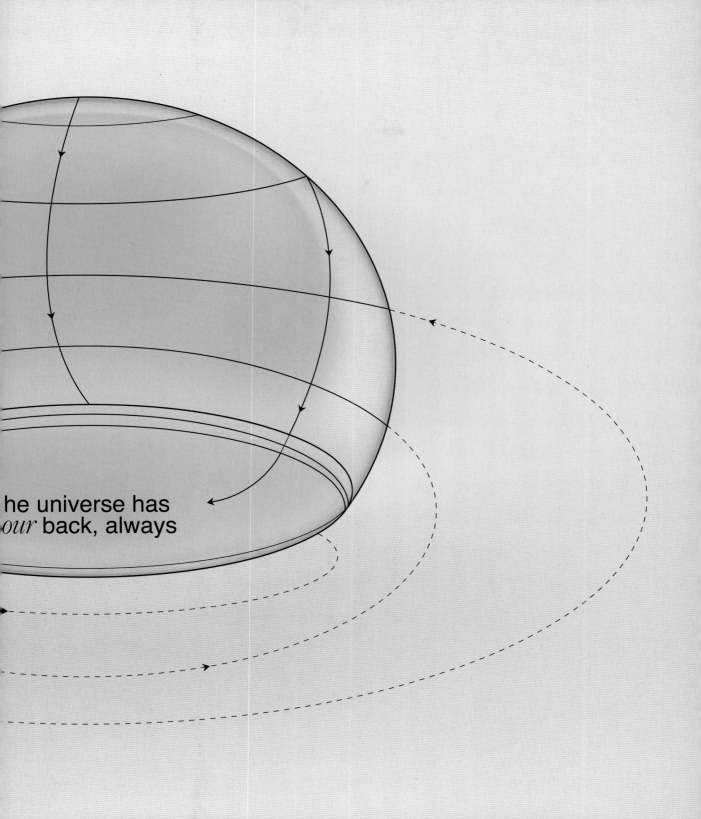

he universe has
our back, always

good things

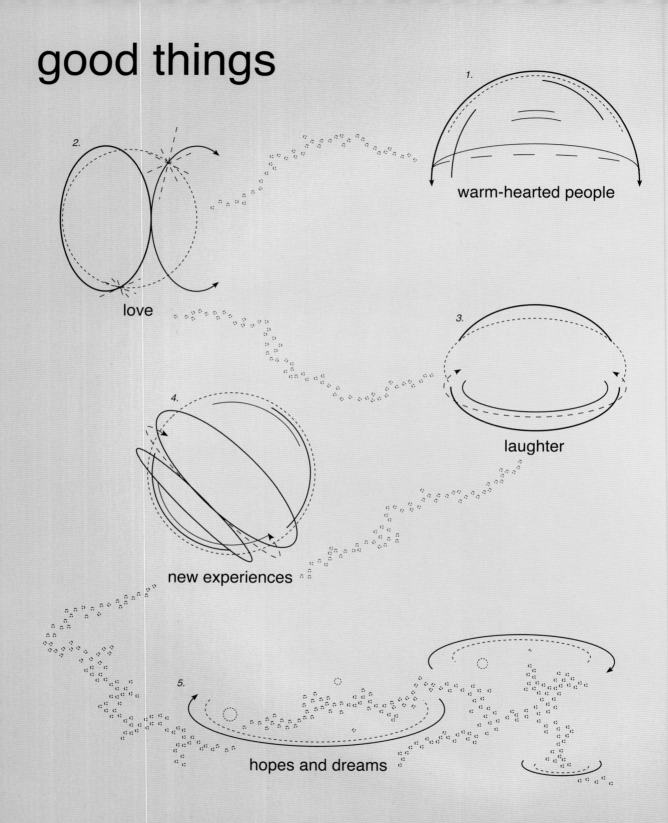

warm-hearted people

love

laughter

new experiences

hopes and dreams

Gratitude for life's blessings

1. Take a moment each day to reflect on three things you're grateful for. You can do this in your mind or say them out loud.

2. When you wake up in the morning, set an intention for the day. This could be something like, "I intend to find joy in the small things today."

3. Throughout the day, make a conscious effort to notice the good things around you. This could be the beauty of nature, the kindness of a stranger, or the love of your family and friends.

4. In the evening, reflect on your day and acknowledge the moments of joy and gratitude you experienced.

5. Before you go to sleep, take a few deep breaths and visualize the good things in your life. Focus on feeling joy, gratitude, and contentment.

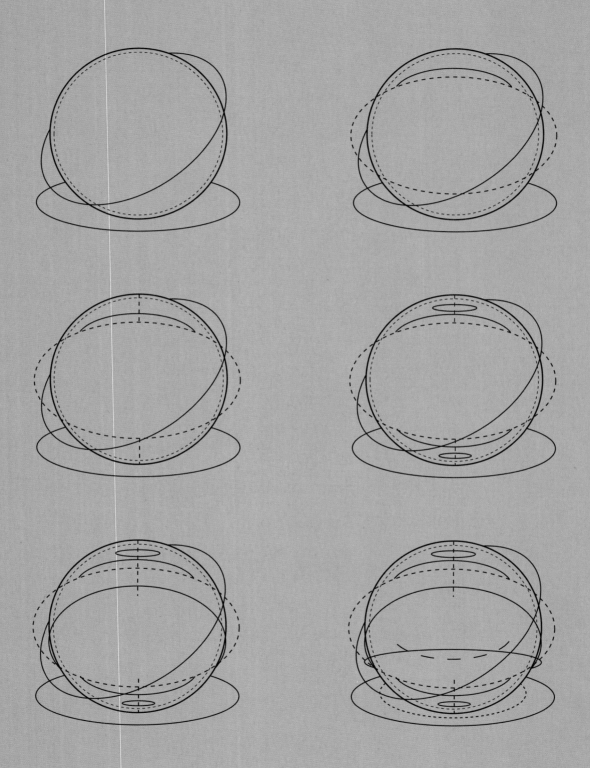

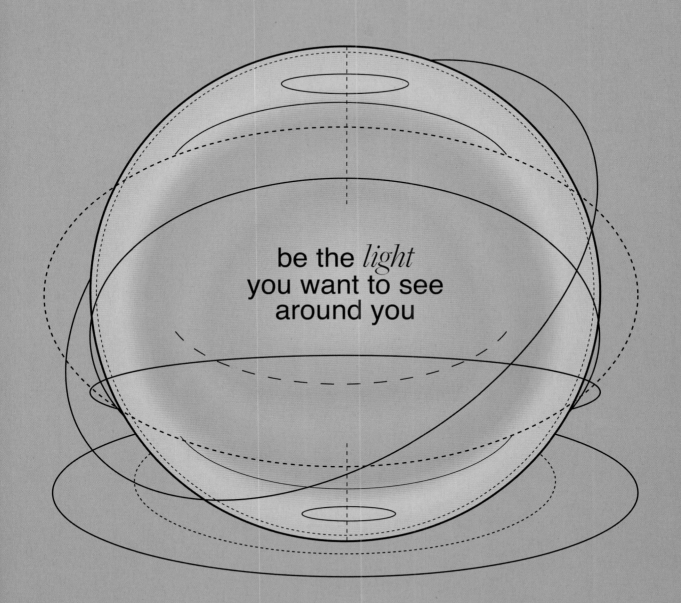

be the *light*
you want to see
around you

Letting go

1. Find a quiet space and grab a pen and paper or open a blank document.

2. Write a letter releasing any thoughts, emotions, or situations you want to let go of.

3. Express your feelings honestly and openly, acknowledging their impact on you.

4. Forgive yourself and others involved, offering compassion and understanding.

5. Reflect on the lessons learned and how they have shaped you.

6. End the letter with words of closure and release, embracing a future filled with peace.

7. Decide whether to keep the letter as a symbol of the power of release or ceremoniously destroy it to signify letting go.

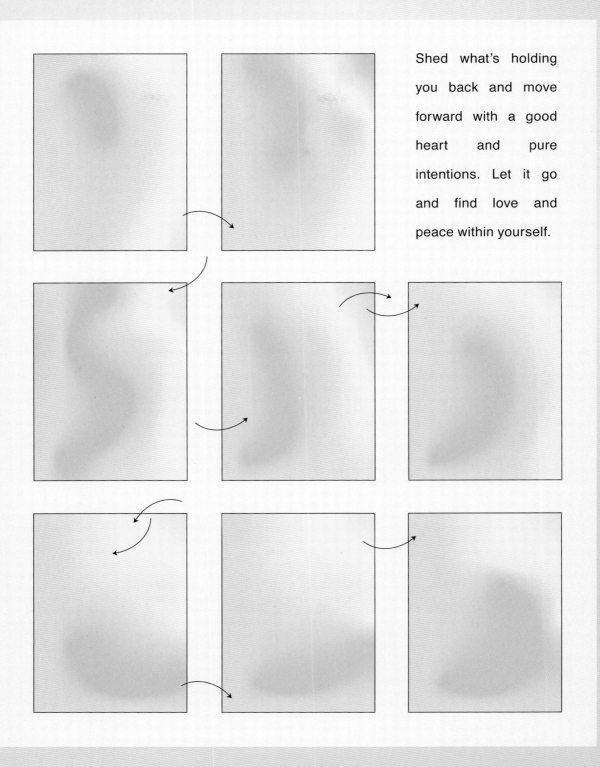

Shed what's holding you back and move forward with a good heart and pure intentions. Let it go and find love and peace within yourself.

morning affirmations

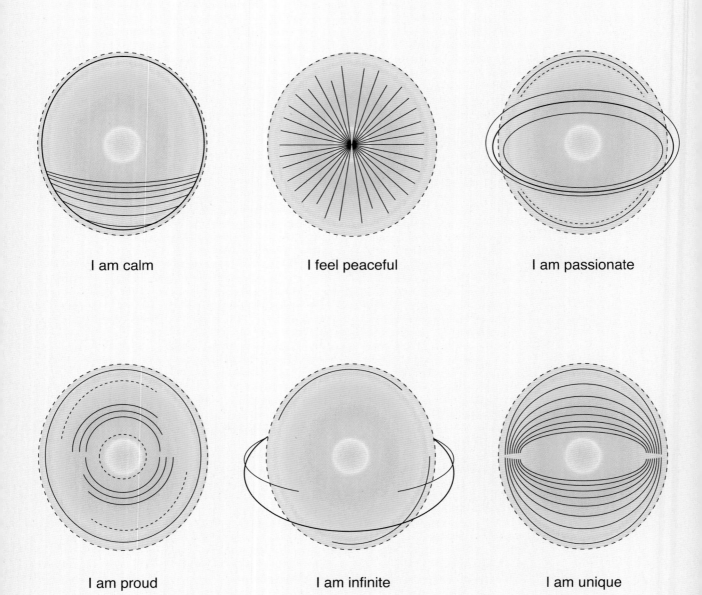

I am calm

I feel peaceful

I am passionate

I am proud

I am infinite

I am unique

evening affirmations

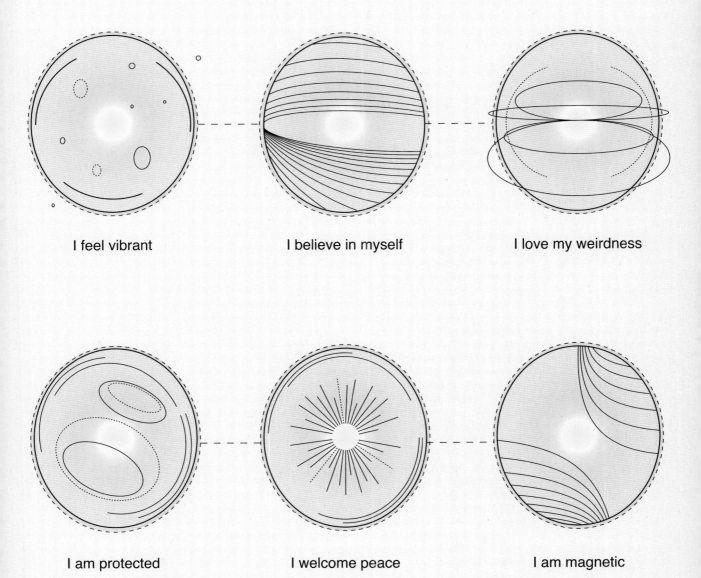

I feel vibrant

I believe in myself

I love my weirdness

I am protected

I welcome peace

I am magnetic

try to be *an observer*
so that the outside world doesn't
affect your peace of mind

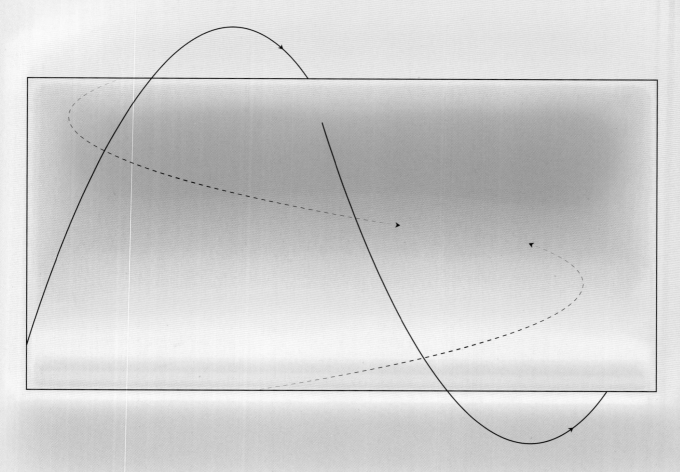

observe the world
around you

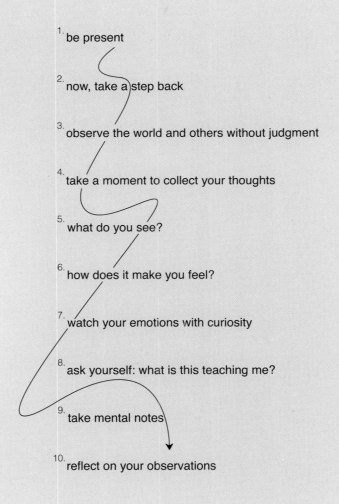

1. be present

2. now, take a step back

3. observe the world and others without judgment

4. take a moment to collect your thoughts

5. what do you see?

6. how does it make you feel?

7. watch your emotions with curiosity

8. ask yourself: what is this teaching me?

9. take mental notes

10. reflect on your observations

life is a series of sunsets and sunrises,

each one bringing its own unique beauty and change

the greatest
adventure is
life *itself*

with *optimism*,
there is always
a way forward

little
things to
remember

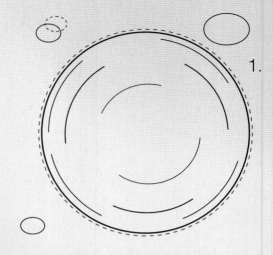

1.

allow the universe
to do its thing

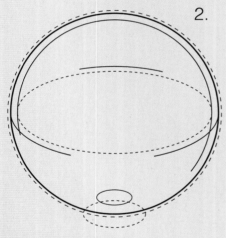

2.

your uniqueness
is your power

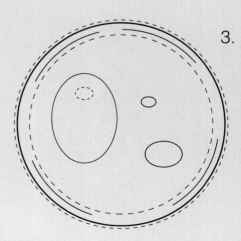

3.

protect your peace
and energy

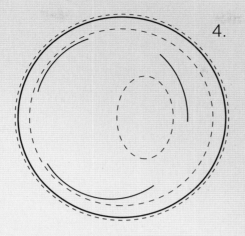

4.

trust that it will
happen at the right time

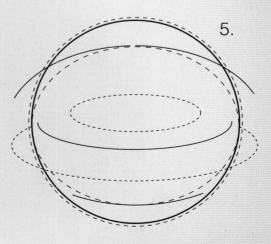

5.

you are doing great

today's **affirmations**

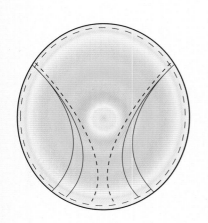

I am aligned

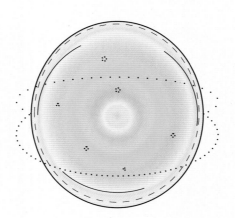

I am calm

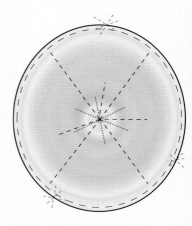

I am present

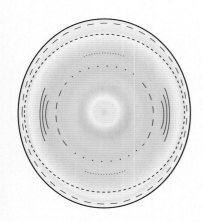

I am loving

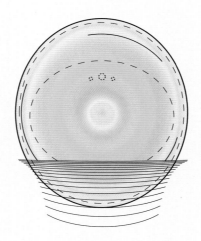

I am confident

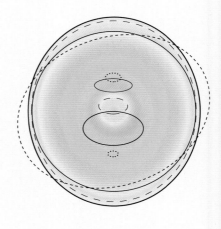

I am joyful

I am . . .

hold on to *hope*

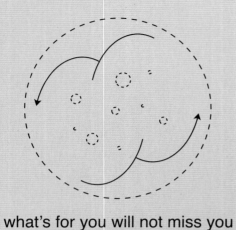

what's for you will not miss you

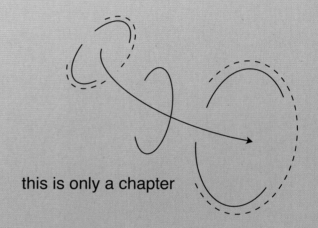

this is only a chapter

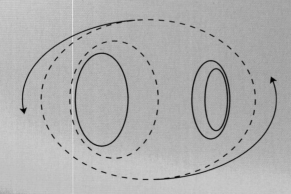

new opportunities are coming

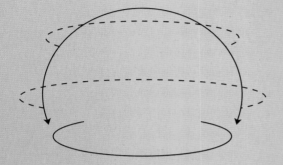

the sun will rise again

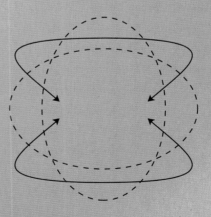

the universe has your back

play good music

soak up sunlight

breathe

shift your energy

release emotions
(cry, laugh, scream)

move your body

journal

make
space
for

healing

things
that matter

joy

the life
you want

gratitude

new
beginnings

romanticize

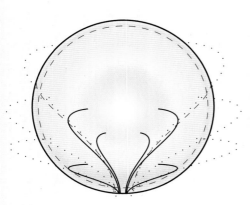

buy yourself flowers

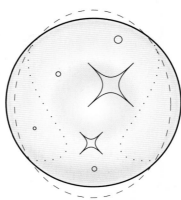

go to a bookshop

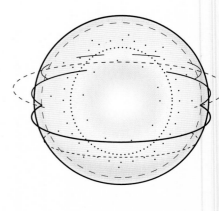

eat your favorite pastry

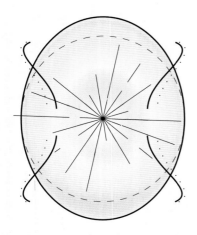

sit in the sun

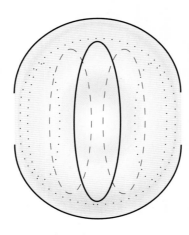

spend time in nature

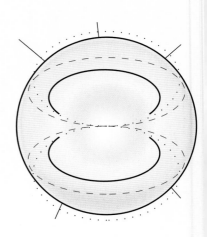

do something creative

your day

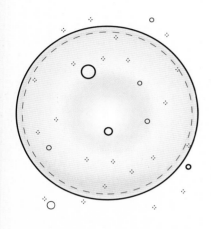

light the fireplace

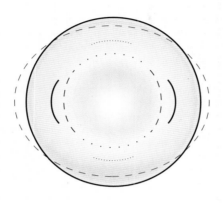

make yourself some tea

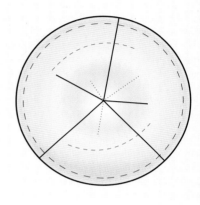

plan a picnic

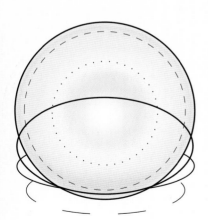

go for a bike ride

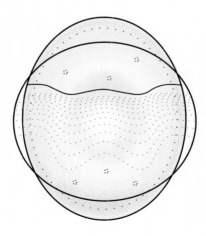

swim in the ocean/lake

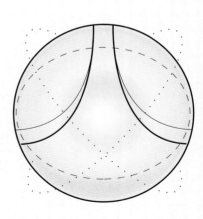

explore new places

little things that *matter*

1.

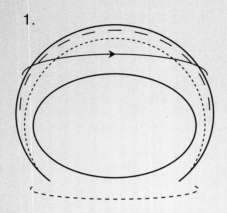

a kind and genuine smile

2.

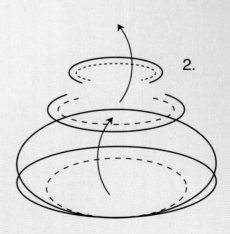

handwritten notes

3.

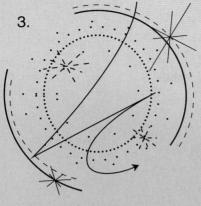

enjoying the present

4.

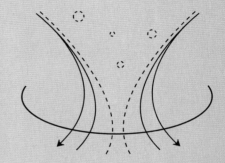

long conversations

5.

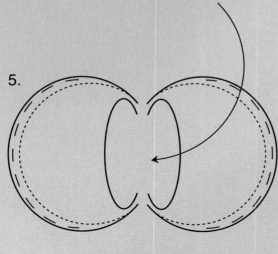

a helping hand

enjoy the
present

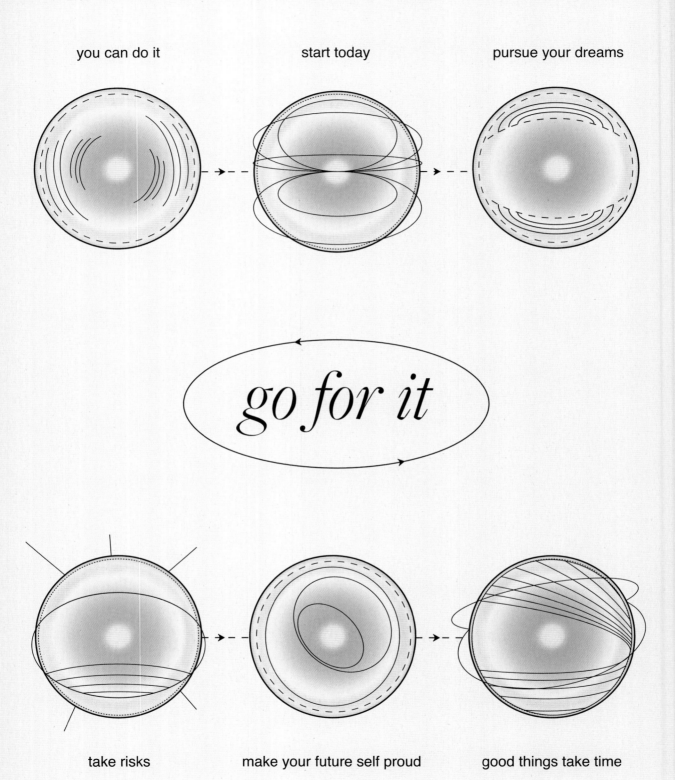

you can do it

start today

pursue your dreams

go for it

take risks

make your future self proud

good things take time

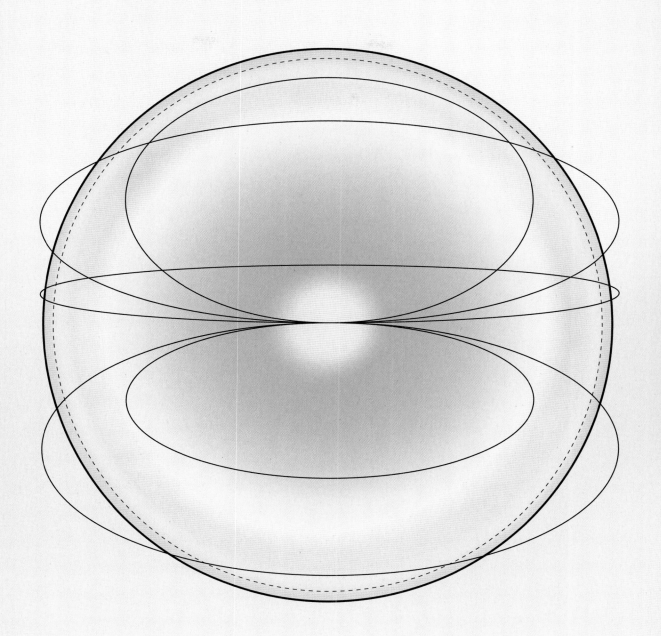

repeat
after me

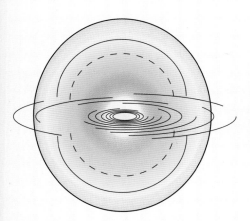

I follow my heart

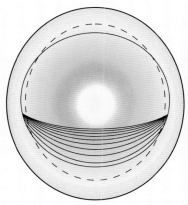

I am light

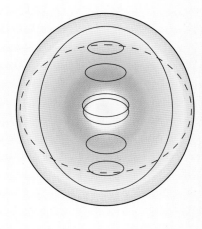

I continually grow

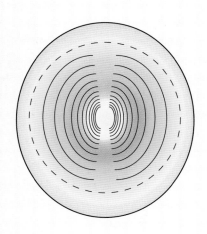

I choose joy

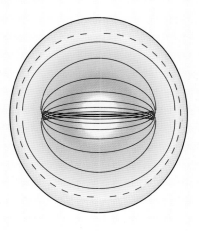

I am love

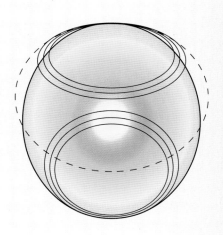

I feel empowered

Chapter 4

Growth

The journey of evolving and growing takes courage, dedication, patience, and a willingness to challenge ourselves. It requires shedding old, limiting beliefs, behaviors, and patterns and embracing new ways of thinking, feeling, and being. Transformation can sometimes be disorienting or scary, but the rewards are significant. Every step in the process can lead to a more fulfilling and meaningful life.

This path of growth is a continuous journey, without a fixed endpoint. It's an ongoing process of self-discovery, learning, and evolving. Each journey is unique, and there is no right or wrong way to approach it. Understanding that our evolution is never complete allows us to stay curious and open, leading to opportunities for connection, beauty, and possibility at every turn.

blooming **is**

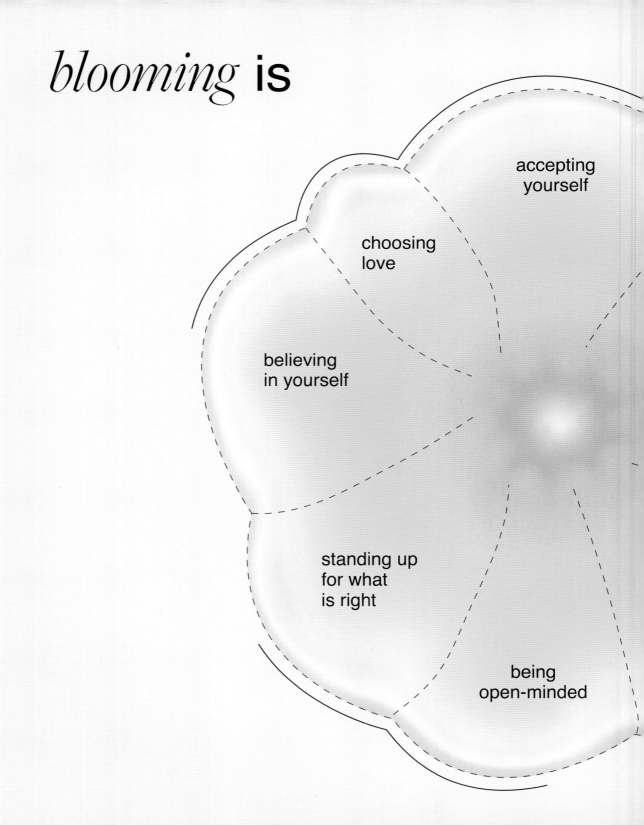

accepting
yourself

choosing
love

believing
in yourself

standing up
for what
is right

being
open-minded

146

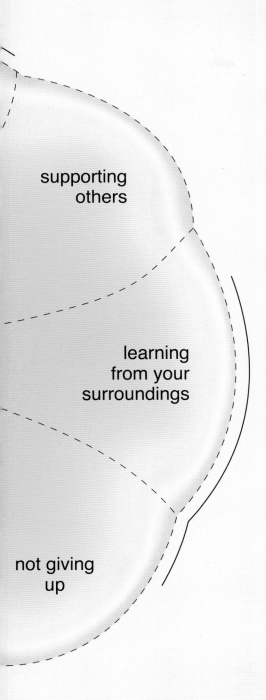

supporting
others

learning
from your
surroundings

not giving
up

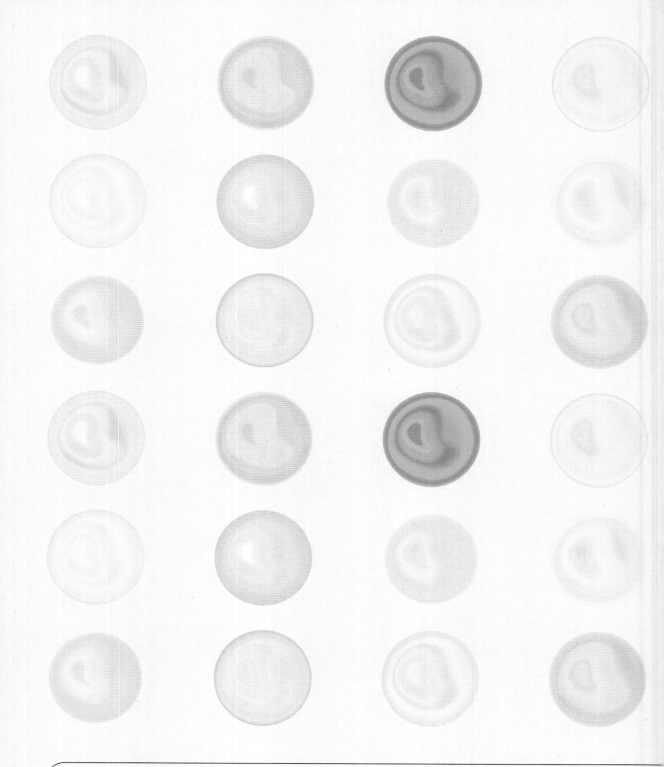

evolving means · · · · · · · · · · · · courage · · · · · · · · · · · · acceptance · · · · · · · · · · · · u

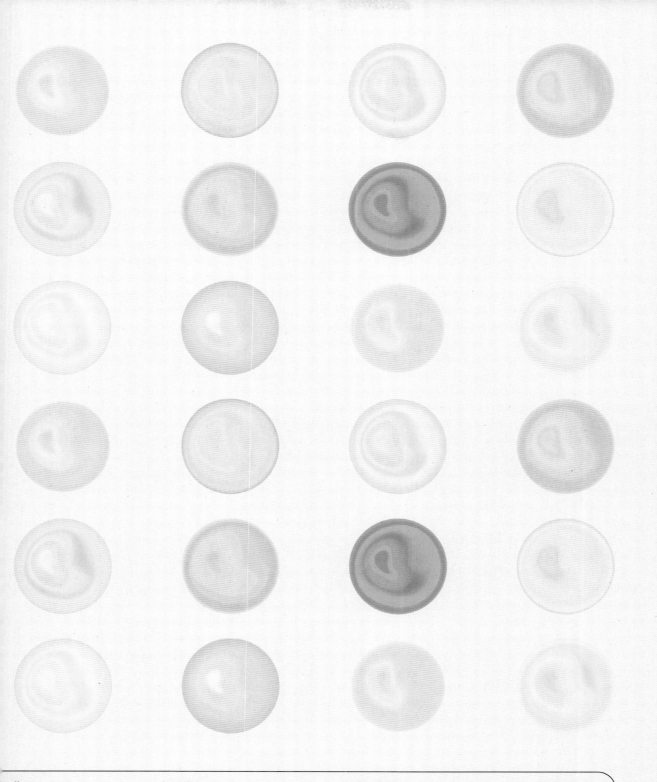

nding · · · · · · · · · · · · · · · · · healing · · · · · · · · · · · · · · · · · changing · · · · · · · · · · · · · · · · · growing

149

you *have* time

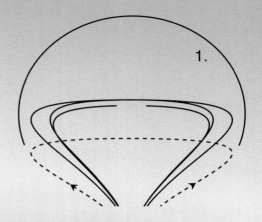

flowers need time to bloom

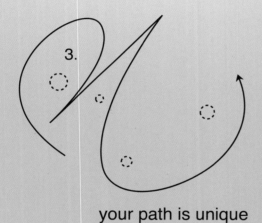

your path is unique

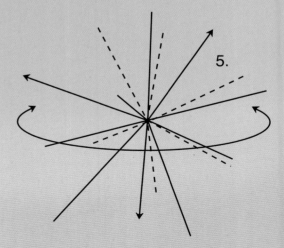

in the end, everything will be OK

2.

take it day by day

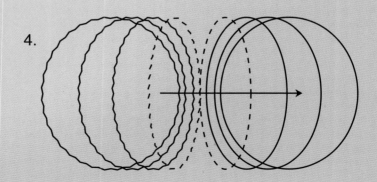

4.

replace negative thoughts with uplifting ones

breathe in....

1

3

calm

your mind

breathe out

3

1

breathe in the new day

brew your favorite beverage
and sit outside for a few minutes

daily morning practice

watch as the colors of the sky change
and listen to the sounds of the birds

take time to watch the world come
to life and to be fully present

self-care is

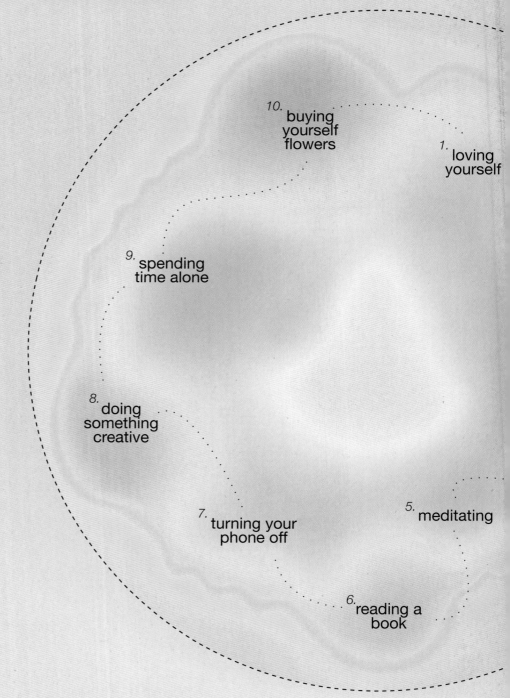

10. buying
yourself
flowers

1. loving
yourself

9. spending
time alone

8. doing
something
creative

5. meditating

7. turning your
phone off

6. reading a
book

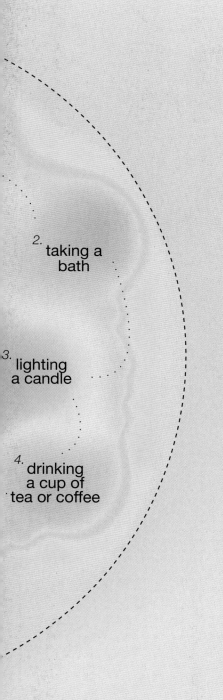

2. taking a
   bath

3. lighting
   a candle

4. drinking
   a cup of
   tea or coffee

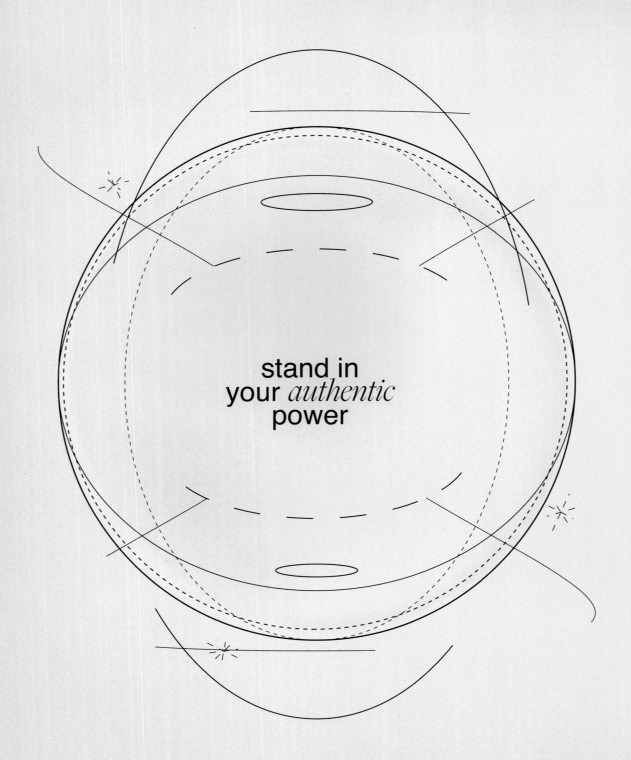

stand in
your *authentic*
power

Ground yourself and find stability

1. Find a place to stand or sit comfortably
   with your feet on the ground,
   and imagine that you are a tree

2. Focus on your feet
   and become aware of how they feel

3. Visualize roots growing
   from your feet into the ground,
   anchoring you firmly

4. Feel the sensation of the roots
   going deeper into the earth

5. Gently move your attention upward through your body,
   imagining your legs and torso as a strong
   and steady tree trunk

6. Take three deep breaths;
   feel how rooted and anchored you are

7. Carry this sense of stability
   with you as you move through your day

we are all on the same journey
to uncover, discover, and
realize the same *truths*

1. print photos of people/moments you are grateful for

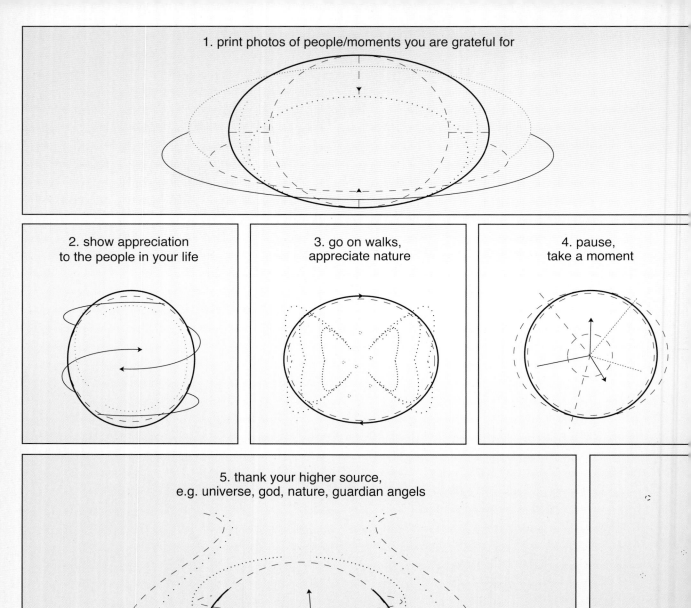

2. show appreciation to the people in your life

3. go on walks, appreciate nature

4. pause, take a moment

5. thank your higher source, e.g. universe, god, nature, guardian angels

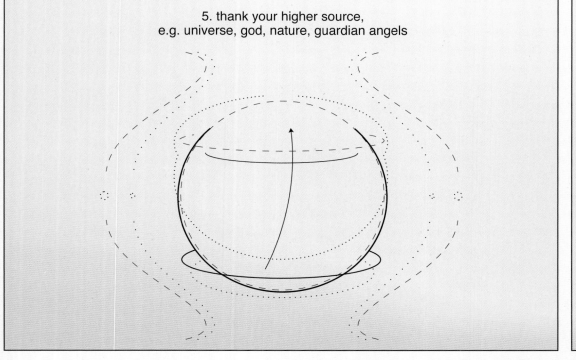

6. keep a gratitude journal

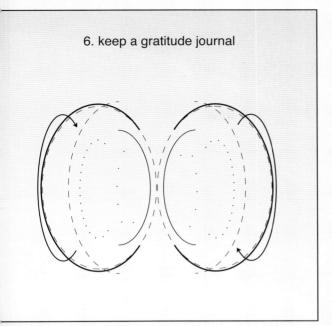

7. use mantras to shift your focus

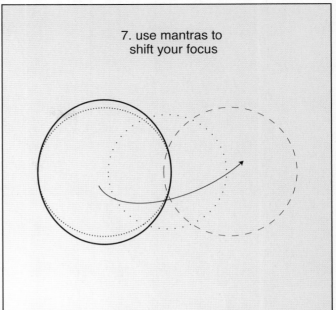

gratitude practices

8. keep gratitude cards, when you need a boost, pull out a note as a reminder

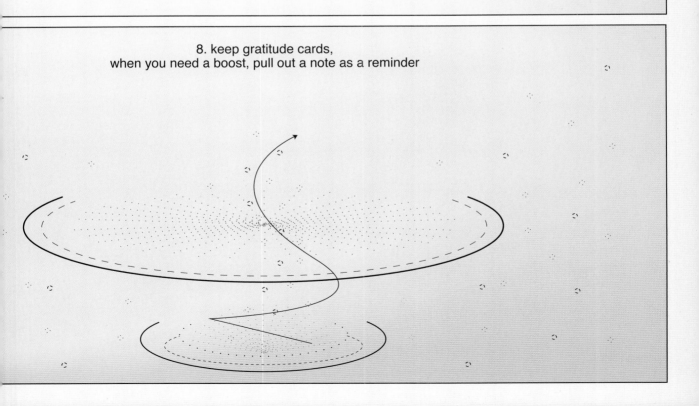

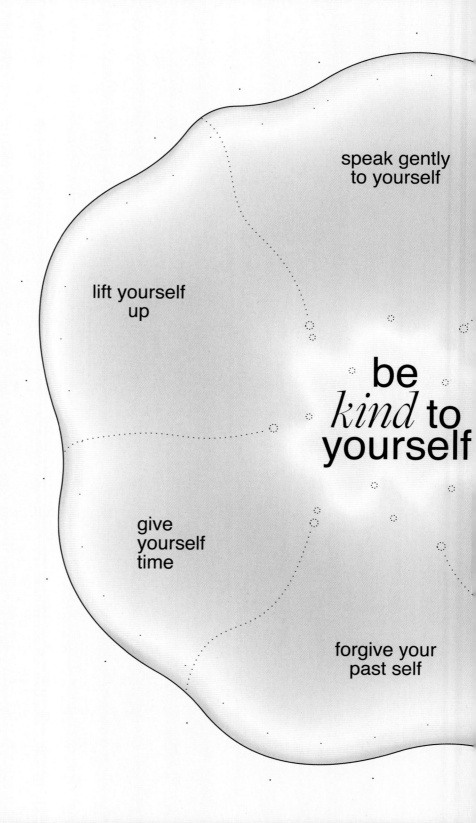

speak gently
to yourself

lift yourself
up

be
kind to
yourself

give
yourself
time

forgive your
past self

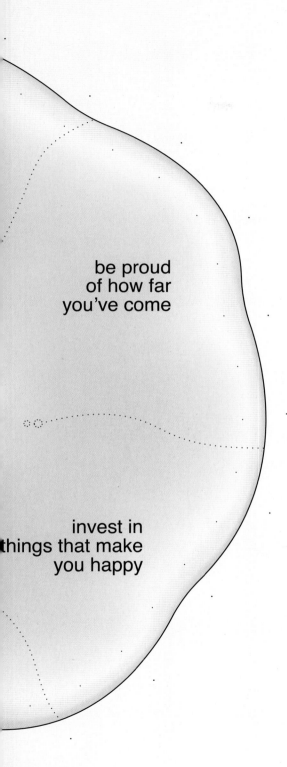

be proud
of how far
you've come

invest in
things that make
you happy

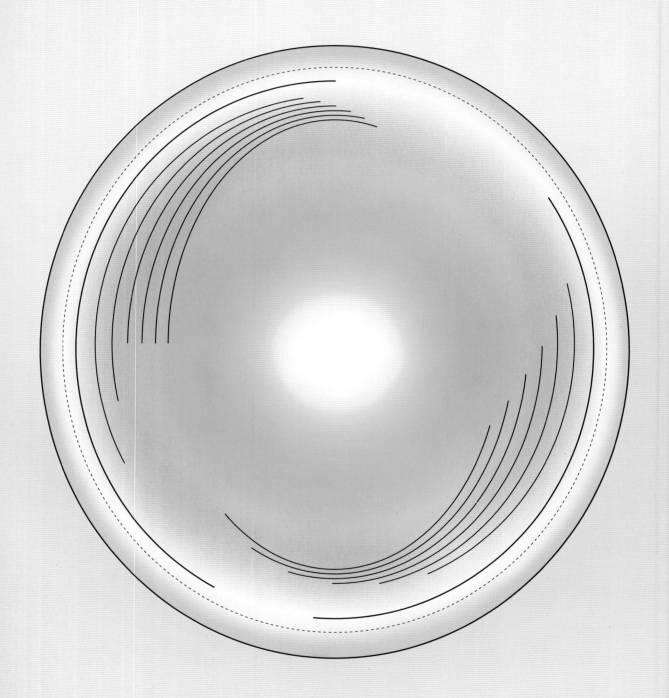

good news

you are doing
amazing

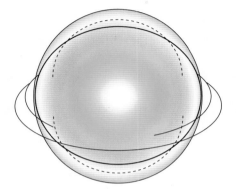

manifestation
is real

you create
your future

others' perception
is their reflection

love will
always win

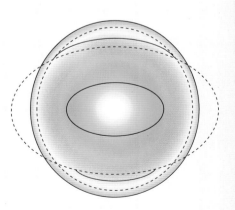

it will all work out
in the end

1. be the warm light
2. be the gentle light
3. be the hopeful light
4. be the kind light

1.

3.

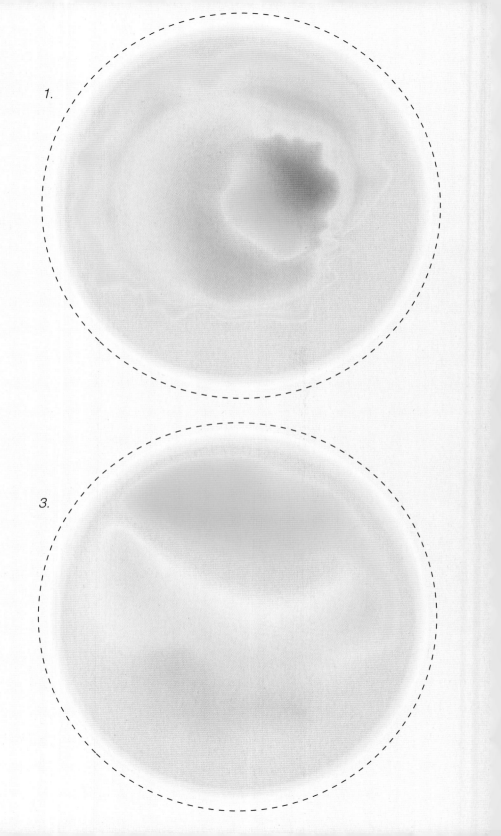

2.

4.

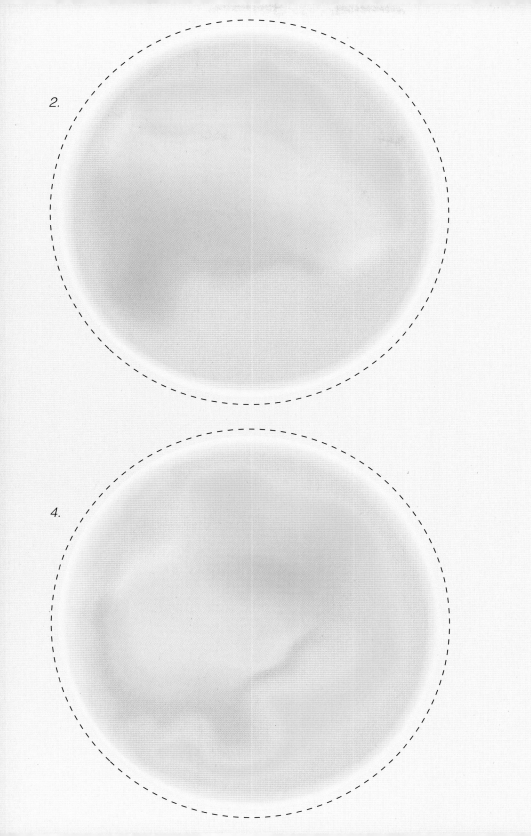

1. breathe

2. be thankful

3. calm your mind

4. love today
repeat

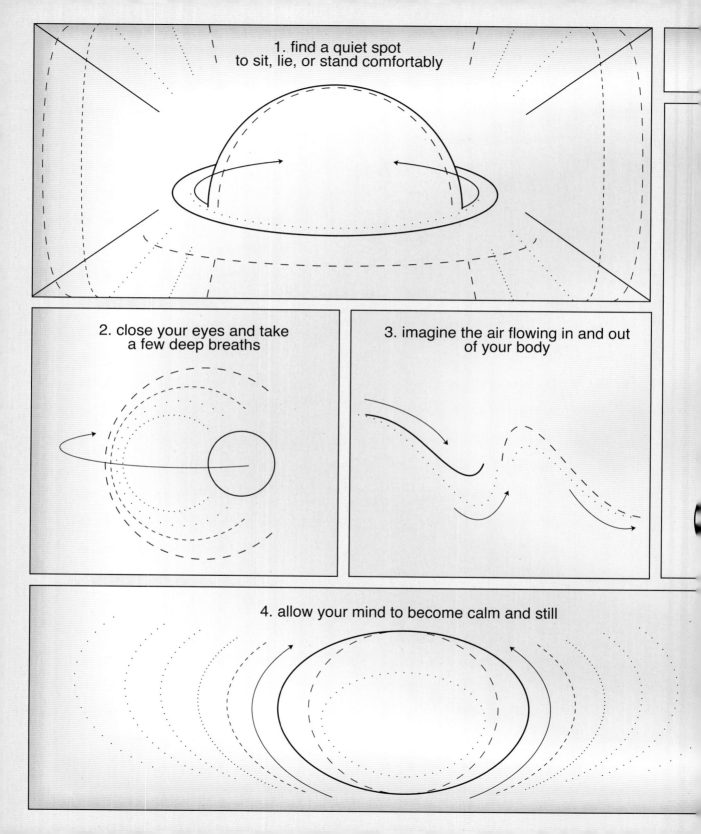

1. find a quiet spot
to sit, lie, or stand comfortably

2. close your eyes and take
a few deep breaths

3. imagine the air flowing in and out
of your body

4. allow your mind to become calm and still

5. if your mind starts to wander,
ring your focus back to your breath

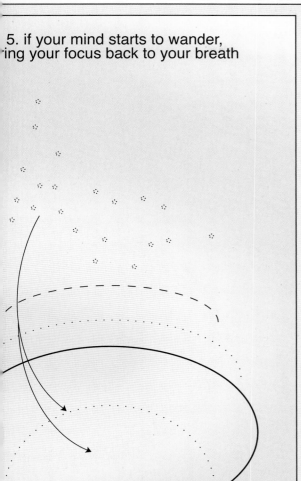

6. keep your attention on your breath

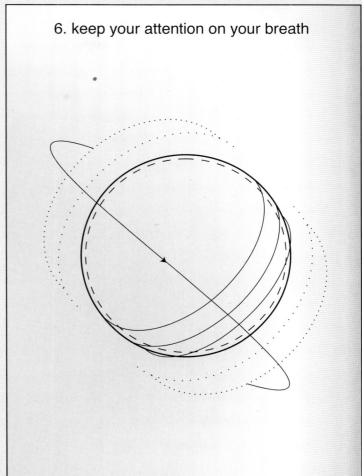

7. when you're ready,
open your eyes

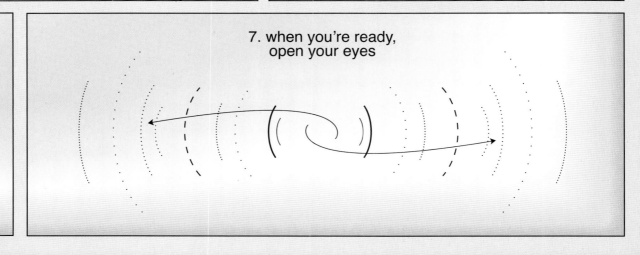

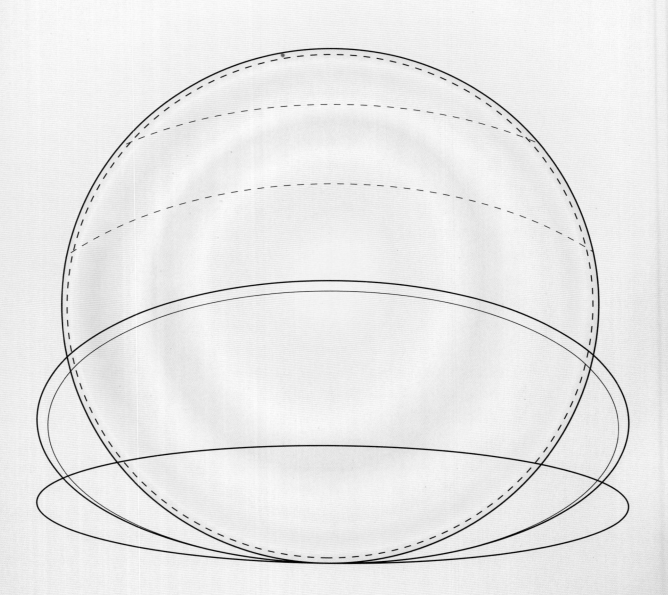

show others that
there is love here

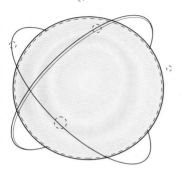

put smiles
on faces

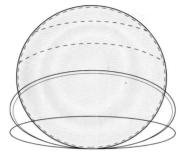

light up
their hearts

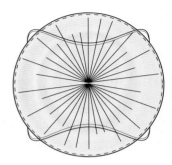

kindness
changes
everything

brighten up
someone's day today

use your gifts
to spread light

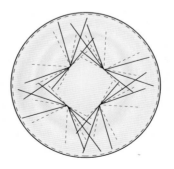

every little act
matters

Chapter 5

Hope

In the end, the arc of our journey is simple. We see. We feel. We change. We grow.

As we grow, we gain knowledge that helps us understand the world and ourselves better. We become more compassionate toward ourselves and others. We let go of judgment and embrace acceptance. We experience the peace and contentment that come from being in alignment with our true selves.

When we approach life from this place of clarity, we can see that the world is full of hope and light. And when we hope—when we wish for good things for ourselves and others—we open our hearts to a sense of possibility and become more aware of the magic around us every day, including the magic within us.

I believe that we are all born with a spark of light in our hearts and that when we are able to connect with that light, we can become the best version of ourselves. Our light illuminates the lives of those around us, making the world a more hopeful, beautiful place.

You are here to have an incredible journey. I know that it is not always easy. There may be times when you feel lost, unsure, or overwhelmed, but remember that your inner light is always shining within you. Let it guide you on your bright, bright journey.

hope is the gentle whisper

that reminds us to hold on

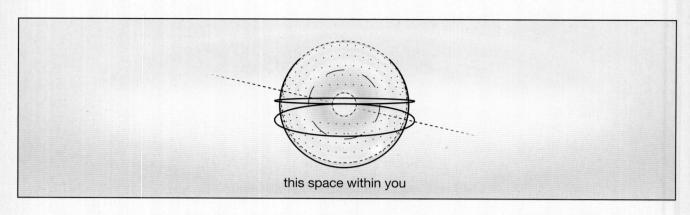

this space within you

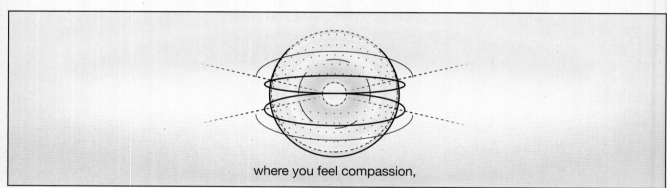

where you feel compassion,

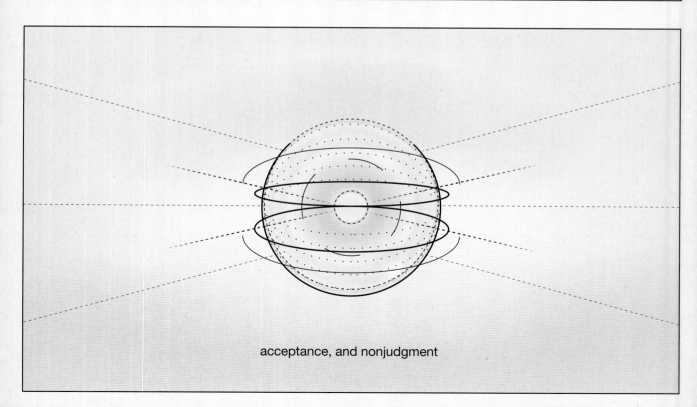

acceptance, and nonjudgment

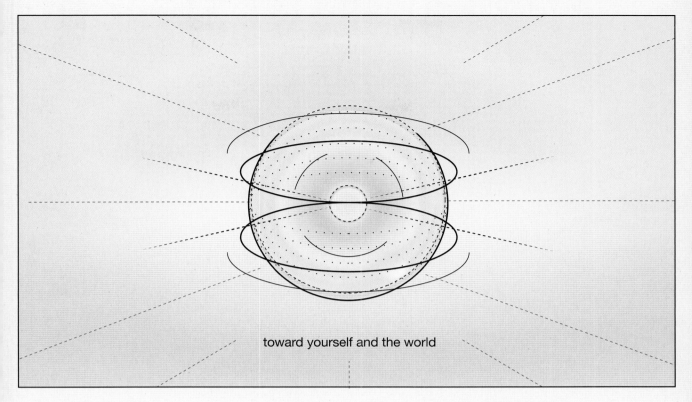

toward yourself and the world

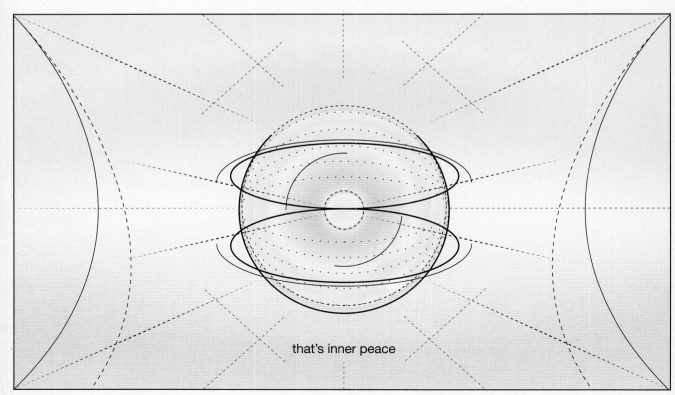

that's inner peace

a message to your
inner child
(say out loud)

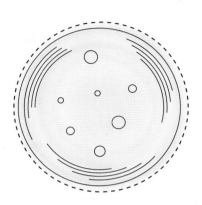

I love you

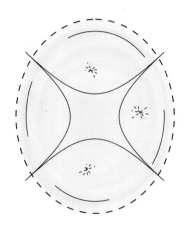

I see you

I hear you

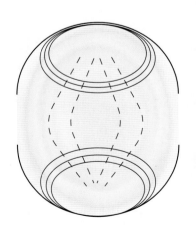

I accept you

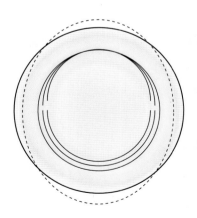

I appreciate you

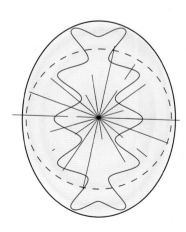

I admire you

How to talk to the universe

1. Choose a peaceful and private location
where you can focus your energy and attention
on connecting with the universe.

2. Share what's happening in your life. Explain both
the positive and challenging aspects of your
current situation.

3. Take a moment to reflect on your actions and decisions.

4. Ask the universe, your higher power, for guidance
with the problems you are facing.

5. If you feel the need, ask for signs or messages. If you
receive one, be grateful for the guidance you received.

6. Trust the universe and have faith that it will guide
you in the most creative and unexpected ways.
Believe that everything will work out for the
highest good.

talk to the universe

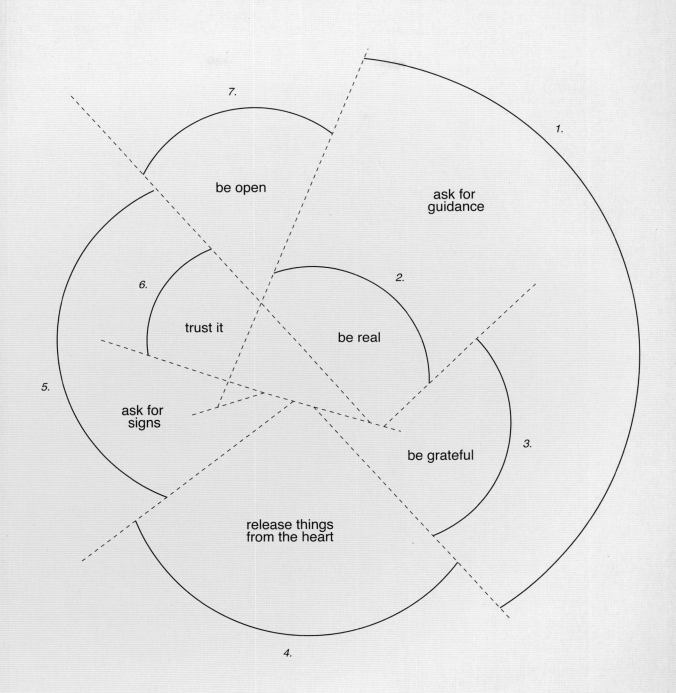

there are

good

things

ahead

things to do to connect to the *universe*

1. see the beauty around you

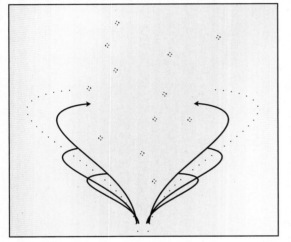

2. watch out for signs

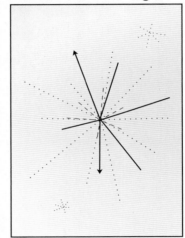

3. talk to the univers

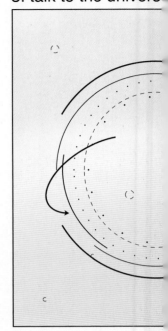

4. manifest your dreams

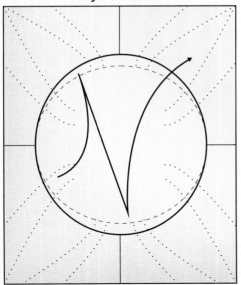

5. walk barefoot

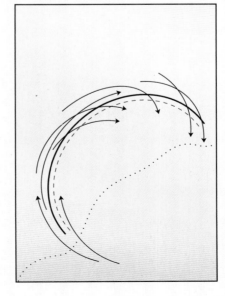

6. enjoy the sun

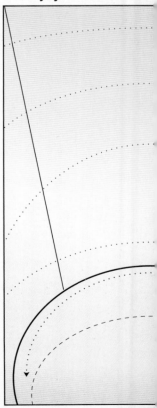

7. be grateful for every day

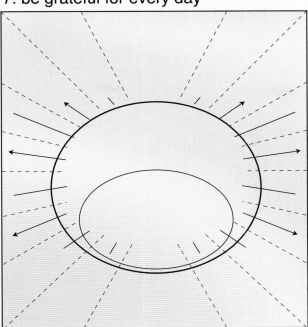

8. meditate

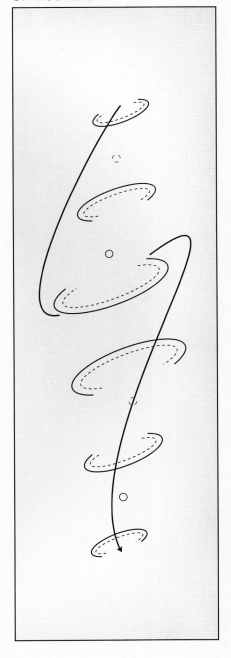

9. open your heart

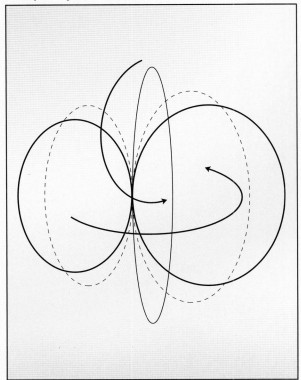

The protective bubble

1. Imagine a bubble of light surrounding you, starting from your head down to your toes.

2. Visualize the bubble as a glowing shield of energy that protects you from negative thoughts, situations, emotions, or energy around you.

3. Picture the bubble expanding wider and wider, embracing everything and everyone you care about, including your home and loved ones.

4. See the bubble as a force that repels negative influences and attracts positive energy and opportunities in life.

5. When you feel ready, express gratitude to your bubble for providing you with protection and positivity.

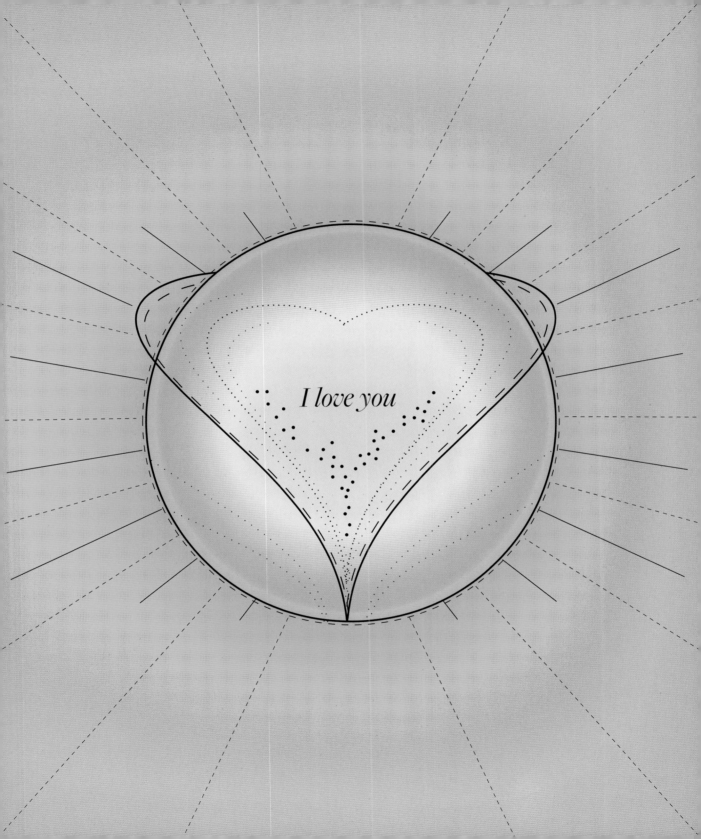

we are light
we are love

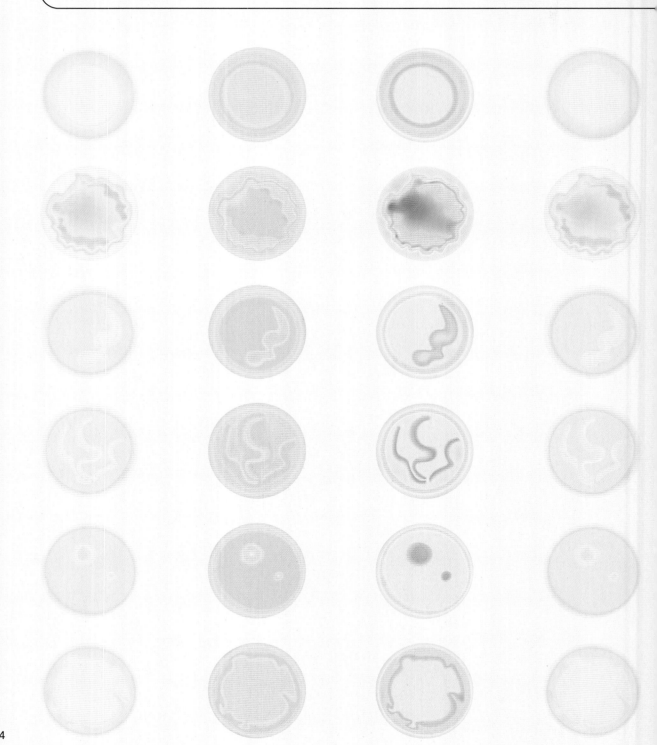

al – – – – – – – – – – – – – – – inspire – – – – – – – – – – – – – attract – – – – – – – – – – – – – radiate

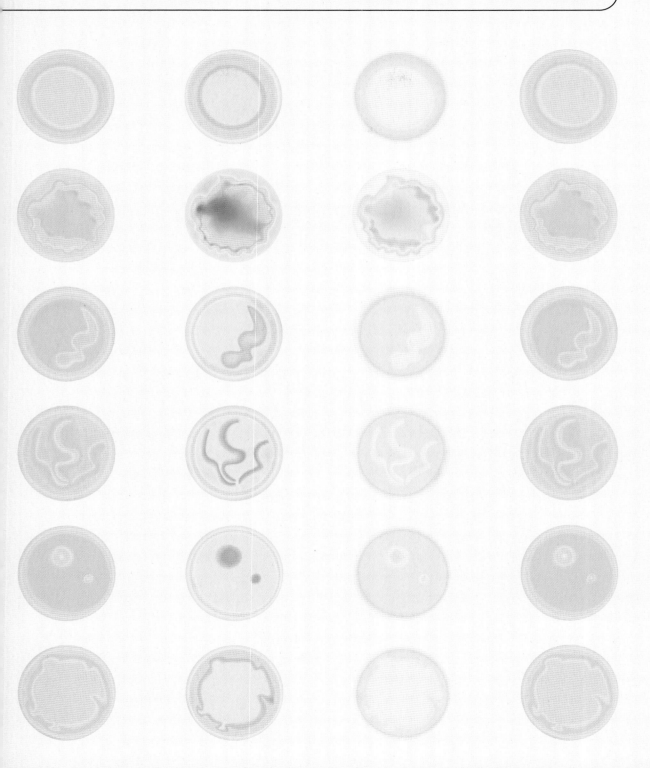

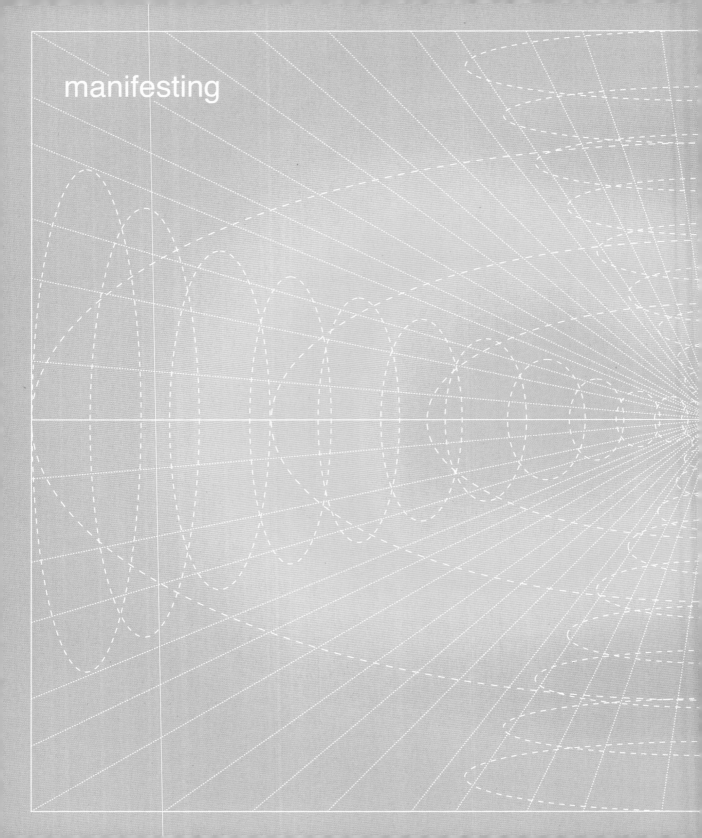

manifesting

how to manifest your goals and dreams

1. gratitude: be thankful for what you already have

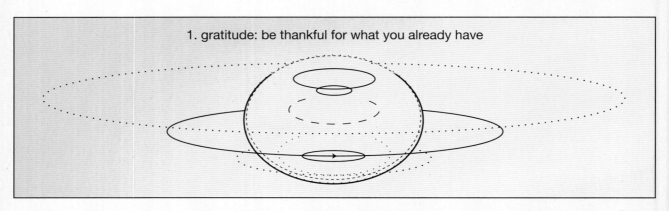

2. desire: know what you want

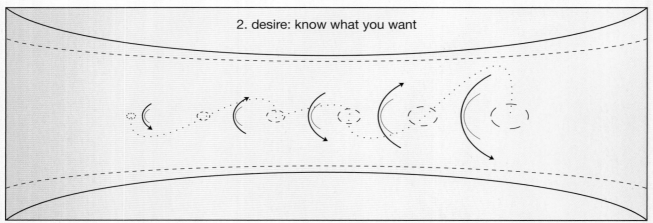

3. envision: feel as if it already happened

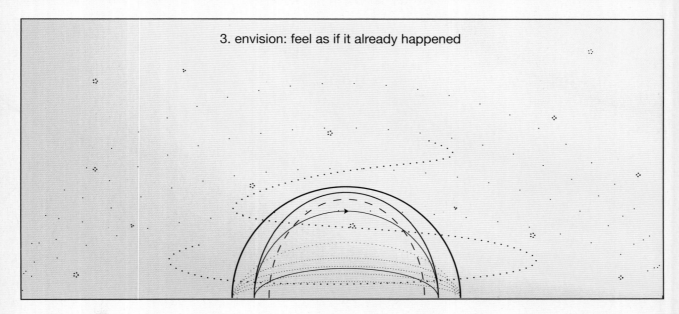

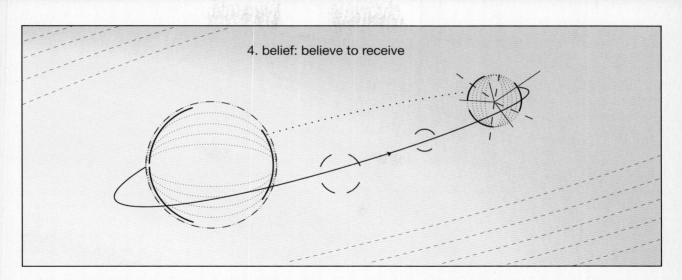

4. belief: believe to receive

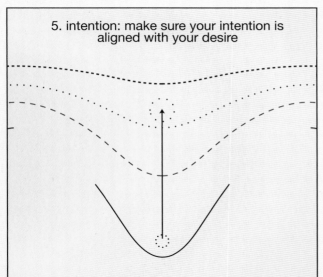

5. intention: make sure your intention is aligned with your desire

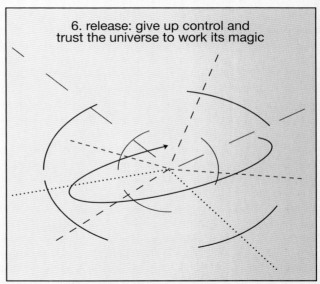

6. release: give up control and trust the universe to work its magic

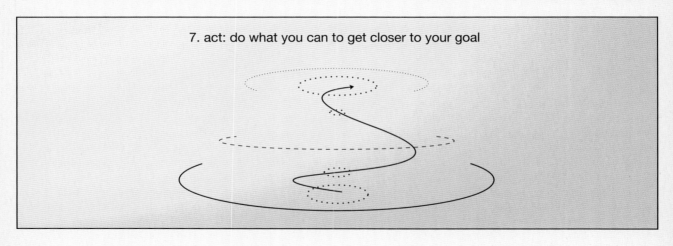

7. act: do what you can to get closer to your goal

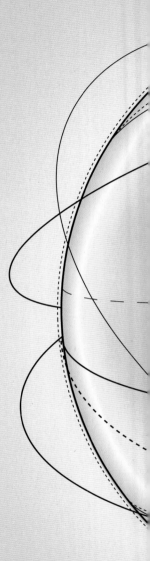

**To build the beautiful life you deserve,
begin by inquiring within:**

What do I envision for my life?
What activities do I love doing?
What sights do I want to see?
What brings me happiness?
What skills am I good at?
What activities give me good energy?
What do I truly desire?

By taking a few minutes to reflect on these questions,
you can gain a better understanding of what brings joy
and fulfillment to your life and take steps to make
it a reality.

create a beautiful life for yourself

an *energized* soul

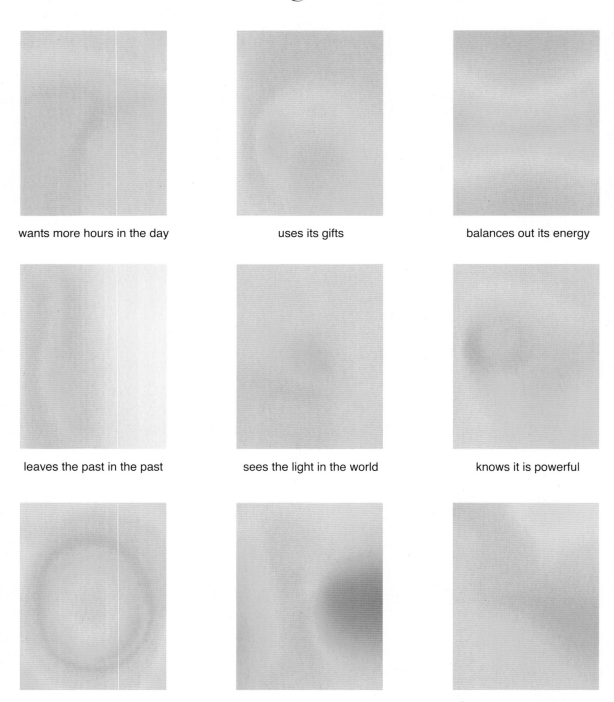

wants more hours in the day

uses its gifts

balances out its energy

leaves the past in the past

sees the light in the world

knows it is powerful

takes accountability for its actions

is open to other perspectives

doesn't believe every thought it has

align yourself by bringing
your thoughts, feelings,
and actions into harmony
with your values and goals

Enjoying your present

1. Take a moment to look around you and notice the beautiful things that surround you—the sights, sounds, and sensations. Where are you right now? What is unique and special about this place and moment?

2. Appreciate the phase of life you are in and be present in it. Recognize the stage of life you are in and be present in it. Appreciate the long journey that led you here. Time moves quickly, so cherish each day.

3. Make a list of your dreams and aspirations for this year. What experiences do you want to have? What do you want to create? What new skills or knowledge do you want to gain? What memories do you want to make?

4. Let go of the past and forgive yourself for any mistakes or regrets. Learn from those experiences and focus on what you know now to move forward.

5. Choose happiness by having a positive outlook on life. Stay optimistic and focus on the good things. Remember, every day is a gift.

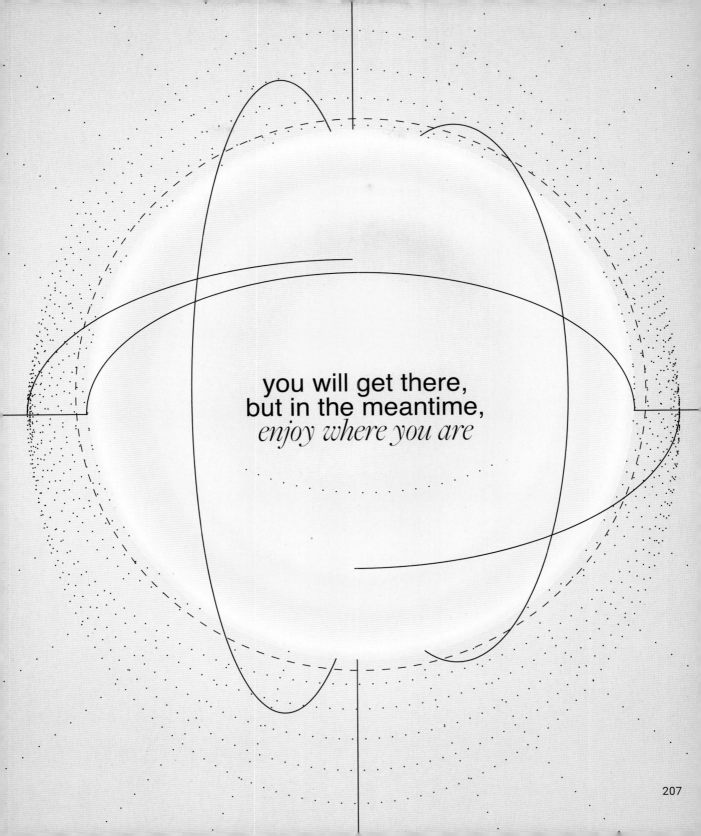

you will get there,
but in the meantime,
enjoy where you are

love languages

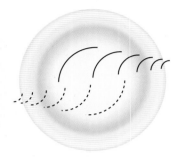

quality time

laughter

sharing music

honesty

positive energy

vulnerability

compassion

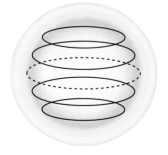

trust

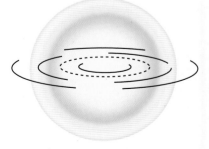

kindness

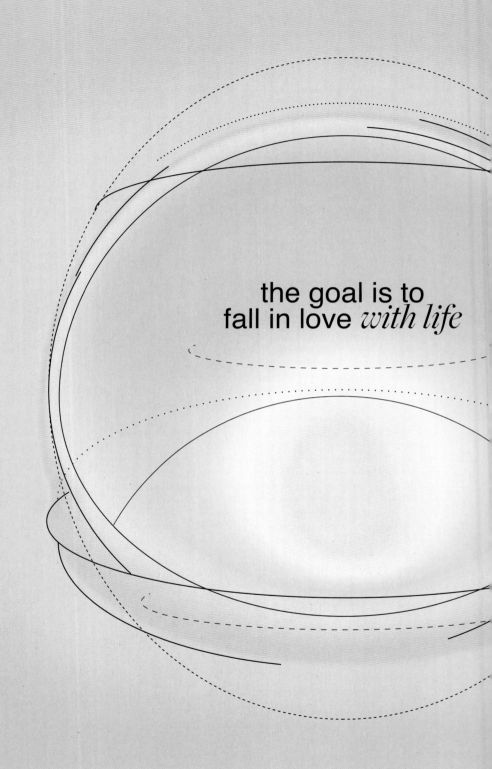

the goal is to
fall in love *with life*

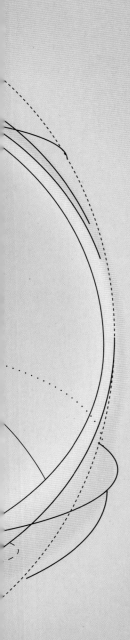

there are
always

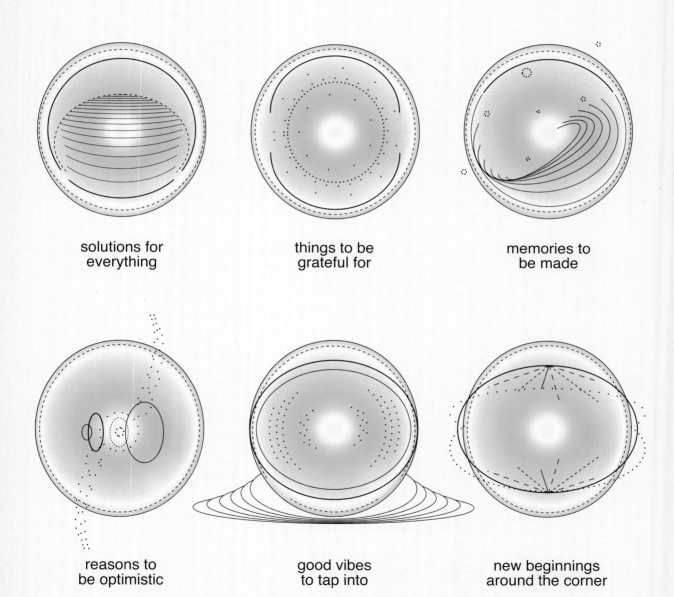

solutions for
everything

things to be
grateful for

memories to
be made

reasons to
be optimistic

good vibes
to tap into

new beginnings
around the corner

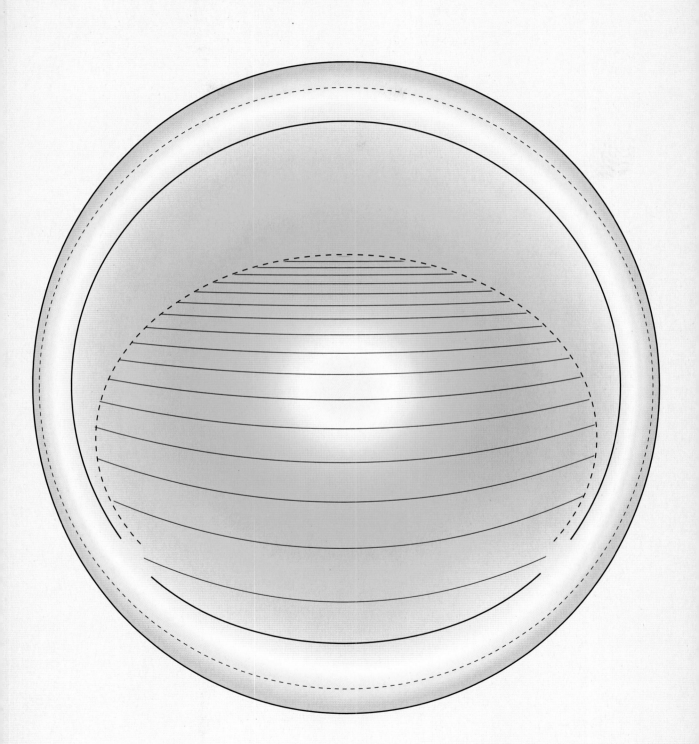

the beauty you see in everything
already exists within you

embrace hope as

your guiding light

the *vibes*

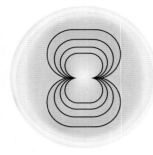

peace and quiet

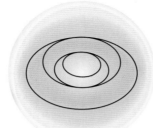

open-minded communication

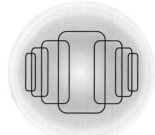

good karma

nature

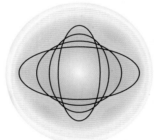

good music

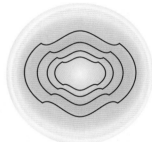

self-awareness

manifestation

great people

journaling

lead with

grace

excitement

sensitivity

respect

understanding

patience

self-worth

authenticity

inner knowledge

the world is full of magic—
all you have to do is connect with it

the most beautiful thing
is to choose happiness every day

every end

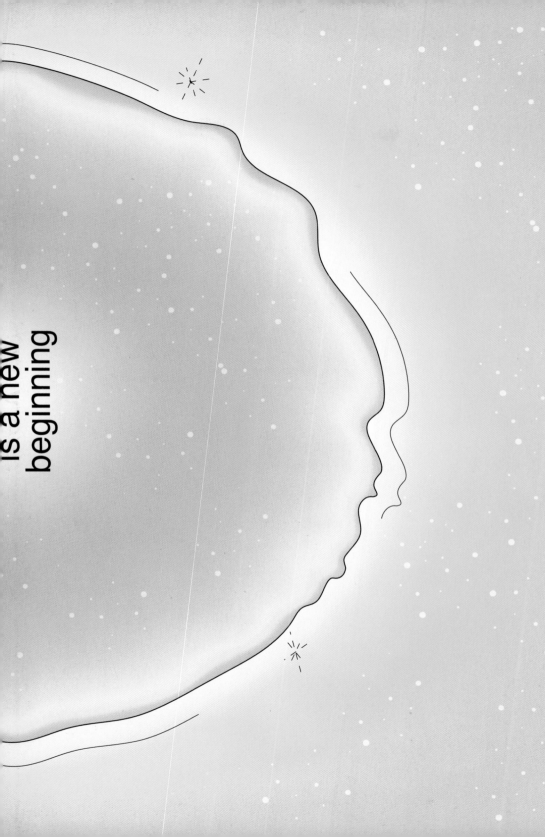